Presented To:

From:

Date:

EVIDENCE

— *of* —

GRACE

EVIDENCE

— *of* —

GRACE

THE IMPERFECT JOURNEY TO PERFECTION

RAYMOND J. MOORE

DESTINY IMAGE® PUBLISHERS, INC.

P.O. Box 310, Shippensburg, PA 17257-0310

"Speaking to the Purposes of God for This Generation and for the Generations to Come."

This book and all other Destiny Image, Revival Press, MercyPlace, Fresh Bread, Destiny Image Fiction, and Treasure House books are available at Christian bookstores and distributors worldwide.

For a U.S. bookstore nearest you, call 1-800-722-6774.
For more information on foreign distributors, call 717-532-3040.
Reach us on the Internet: www.destinyimage.com.

ISBN 13 TP: 978-0-7684-3758-4
ISBN 13 Ebook: 978-0-7684-9003-9

For Worldwide Distribution, Printed in the U.S.A.

1 2 3 4 5 6 7 8 9 10 11 / 13 12 11

DEDICATION

To my wife, who stood by me when it wasn't easy, I want to dedicate this book to you and to say thank you! You are truly a virtuous woman, wife, and mother; I call you blessed. God gave me you because He knew in advance what I was going to go through and that I would need someone like you. I love you dearly!

I would also like to dedicate this book to those who are continuing their journey in spite of all the setbacks that could have caused you to detour.

ACKNOWLEDGMENTS

I want to thank my Lord and Savior Jesus Christ for His long-suffering toward me, for His goodness, grace, and stubborn redeeming love. I also would like to (without listing numerous names) sincerely thank some dear friends who, even when I gave them reasons to doubt me, still believed in God for me. You were there for me, prayed for and encouraged me, and reassured me of your loving support. Special thanks to my family for loving me non-stop and for praying constantly that God would bring something good out of the pit I found myself in. Thank you! May God's richest blessings be multiplied to you.

CONTENTS

INTRODUCTION

This book is about me and some of the heroes of the Bible who achieved great victories and were used mightily of God—but who also had moments of sinful setbacks. These legendary men and women were powerful, but they were not perfect. They were mighty, but they also sinned and made mistakes. They were faithful, but at times they were faithless and unfaithful.

The Church is very good at welcoming the most violent offenders and sinners who have repented of their sins and turned their lives over to the Lord. But with regard to the saints who are already in the Church, if they fall into sin, the Church often becomes "dumbfounded" and, more often than not, reverts to dismissal in order to show utter disapproval and disassociation with such behaviors!

I want to proclaim that the grace of God is greater than our greatest sins and mistakes! The same God who called, anointed, and empowered David to be king of Israel knew that he would fall into sin—mainly adultery and murder. If David was alive today and did what he did in ancient Israel, he would never again be allowed to minister in our churches. Yet God did not remove him from his position. How do we treat today's Davids? Do we seek their restoration, albeit through discipline and restorative justice?

It seems as if the saints of today have a hard time dealing with those who fall into sin because they fail to remember the other side of many of the great saints in the Bible—and even of themselves. Many people know the David who killed Goliath, but not too many people know the David who committed adultery and murder. Many people know the Moses who led the Israelites out of slavery, but not too many people know the Moses who committed murder. And then there were the lies of the patriarchs and so on.

There are no sinless saints. Some have come to salvation early on in their lives (for example, David), but still fell into sin from time to time. Others were sinners for the greater part of their lives (for example, Rahab) and only came to salvation toward the end.

When the world sees both sides of the saints, their strengths and their weaknesses, their victories and their shortcomings, it will be an assurance that God can and will forgive them and use them just as He did the heroes of the Bible. People won't feel like they've messed up so badly that God is anxious to cast them into hell; instead, they will see that He loves them and will forgive them if they truly repent. They will be able to say, "What He's done for others, He can do for me, too."

We are saints because we believe in and have accepted Jesus Christ; we have confessed our sins, and we are forgiven (reconciled) and born again by the blood of Jesus and the grace of Almighty God—not because we haven't sinned. Why do we make the world think we have it all together and are sinless when we're not? It's time for us to declare both sides of the truth.

Introduction

In the chapters that follow, I will share my personal story as well as the stories of several Bible heroes, revealing both their struggles with sin and their encounters with the redeeming grace of God. I have written these stories in the first person, from the character's perspective, because it makes these heroes seem more like real people like us, which, of course, they were. Though in places I have had to "read between the lines" in order to fill in details, I have kept these narratives as close to the biblical accounts as possible. After each narrative, I have written a commentary relating the story to my story and to lessons for the Church. I pray you are encouraged and challenged by these often untold stories about the other side of our Bible heroes.

CHAPTER 1

RAY'S STORY, PART 1

*Assured of the Landing—Not Fully
Informed About the Journey*

 *Let us draw near with a true heart in full
assurance of faith, having our hearts sprinkled
from an evil conscience and our bodies washed
with pure water. Let us hold fast the confession of
our hope without wavering, for He who promised
is faithful* (Hebrews 10:22-23).

I will never forget the season of my life when I sat alone in a jail cell, crying my heart out and glancing back over my life! I thought to myself, *How did I end up in this place?* I had grown up in the Church and had been a Christian pretty much my whole life. Certainly, I hadn't always been faithful, especially in my teenage years, but I wasn't doing things that could have landed me in jail either. I was a man of the Word who preached and ministered on the worship team at my church, going back and forth between the drums and piano. I was on my way to what I thought was a successful life of ministry. I had just finished Bible college a few months earlier, had accepted a ministry proposal, and was making plans to move to a new town with my wife and daughter to become the youth pastor of a small church.

When the pastor of the church heard what I had done, he immediately canceled the ministry proposal. The Bible college I had been a part of and the church I was attending, not wanting to associate with me in any way, completely abandoned me! I was a wounded soldier who had been left behind and deserted by his comrades—left to die, make it on my own, or suffer at the enemy's discretion.

To me, there was only one option: press through. I knew that the enemy knows no such thing as mercy. He would devour me to the grave if given the opportunity. I was in a time and place that felt like the end of the world—as if my calling and life were coming to an end! But a few faithful saints continued to support me, and most importantly, the Lord had not forsaken me.

I was saddened that I had brought such shame and embarrassment to the church community. I had given the enemy grounds on which to reproach the people of God. It was devastating! All of the misfortunes that I'd experienced in my entire life put together were not as hurtful as the predicament I was now facing! I had nightmares that terrified me and left me shaking in a cold sweat! I cried until I had no more tears to cry.

My bed and my pillow were wet with tears. I could actually relate to David when he said in Psalm 6:6, *"I am weary with my groaning; all night I make my bed swim; I drench my couch with my tears."* Furthermore, I was deeply saddened that I had hurt my wife so much; I had let down my family members and friends, those who were looking up to me for great things in the Lord.

I also grieved for the victim of my most disgusting and ungodly behavior!

My heart was humbled, and I acknowledged my sins and the undesirable publicity I had brought to the church community because of my shameful conduct! I cannot express how much I regret my actions! I am truly repentant and am now reaching out to the Church community, my fellow saints in the Lord, for forgiveness. I am wounded and hurting and still have to deal with the consequences that came about because of my sins. Please don't abandon me anymore! Please forgive me; I need your forgiveness.

Not Good Enough

Many are on the outside looking in and may even desire to be a part of the family of God, but they fear being looked down on. They doubt that they're good enough, and they're right. No one is good enough. But too often we try to make them think that somehow we are.

I know I'm not, and I will not try to convince you of how wonderful a saint I am. Rather, I will show you how sinful a saint I was. Why? For too long the Church and many of its leaders have been portraying the image of perfection to the world. We are not perfect; I am not perfect—not even close. We turn people away with our perfectionism Gospel. But really, the world knows that we're not as perfect as we claim.

We know all too well that apart from the grace of God, the love of God, the righteousness that we receive through faith, and the forgiveness of Christ Jesus, we are wretched and condemned sinners! It is not what we have or haven't done that separates us from the world. It's what Jesus Christ has done for us and the fact that we have believed it, acknowledged it, and confessed it—therefore receiving His salvation, His blessing, His adoption as children, and His declaration that we are righteous saints.

Everyone has a story, and I doubt our stories are all about righteousness, peace, joy, faithfulness, love, and so forth in the Holy Ghost. The idea that someone has a story that does not have any shortcomings, regrets, or embarrassing and shameful moments of sin is quite unrealistic. The Bible says, "…*There is none righteous, no, not one*" (Rom. 3:10). Romans 3:23 also says that "*all have sinned*…."

If we believe these Scriptures to mean what they say, then we must acknowledge that somewhere along the line in every person's journey there is unrighteousness and sin. There is always another side to the great accomplishments and successes that you often hear about in many of the saints' stories.

This book may not be the easiest book to read and embrace, considering some of the disturbing contents of sin, especially in my personal story. Some may even find it controversial or offensive. I wondered if any publishing company would be willing to publish a book like this, but I knew I had to write it and leave what is beyond my control to the Lord. I knew He gave me the grace and told me to write it, and I needed to trust Him to bring something good out of my story, even if it is controversial.

If you do find this book disturbing or offensive, I assure you that it was not my goal, and I do apologize. However, I do believe you will be able to find some diamonds if you can dig through. So if you're willing to be gracious with me, wait until the end before drawing your final analysis.

The Other Side of the Story

I often wonder what would happen if people of great influence who have experienced much success, like Billy Graham, T.D. Jakes, Joel Osteen, Joyce Meyers, Beth Moore, Benny Hinn, and so on, told the other side of their stories (not necessarily what others have done to them, but what they have done—their shortcomings). How would the Church respond? And how would the world respond? Would the world see them as hypocrites, or would they see them as prototypes for change—people who are walking in victory and not in the condemnation of their past, people who have experienced the redeeming grace of God?

Wouldn't the world see these saints as people to whom they can relate and who will be better able to relate to them? Such a revelation would make a whole lot of difference. On the other hand, we don't have to sin in every way like the world in order to relate to them. Jesus didn't, and He was still able to reach out to us (see, for example, the story of the woman at the well in John 4:1-42).

It's never good that the saints fall into sin, but when it happens, it's important that the messy story is told, at least in part. How else will the sinner be able to understand the grace, mercy, justice, and unconditional love of God? Too many baby saints are destroyed because of the imbalanced proclamation of the Gospel, and many sinners are hindered by this one-sided story telling. They're hindered because they think they have to be perfect in order to come—that perfection defines sainthood.

Our positions as saints are not based on our actions, but on His—and on our response to Him. There are countless sinners in the world who are kinder, more loving, more forgiving, and have greater integrity than many saints, but that does not make them saints. A king is still a king, even when he messes up and sins, and saints do not cease being saints the moment they fall into sin. If that were the case, the minute they sinned, they would no longer be saints because their sainthood would be based on their perfection and their ability to maintain a sinless life.

Certainly, the sins of Billy Graham and T.D. Jakes, to name a few, are not as despicable as mine (as you will find out later). Neither is Joyce Meyer's sin as shameful as Rahab's. Maybe all they did was tell a little "white" lie and steal a candy from the store when they were only ten years old. But a lot of sinners out there have done just that, and the devil is riding them like little horses, tormenting them with condemnation and guilt. They have never experienced the liberating peace that's found only in God's grace.

So let me ask my fellow saints this question: Are we making it easier for sinners to come home, or are we making it more difficult? Are we consistently giving them reason to think that we are "high and holy" and that they can't reach up to us—just because we're not willing to humble ourselves and share the other side of our story with them?

I understand that the saints are high because we are seated in heavenly places with Christ (see Eph. 2:6). I also know that the saints are holy because we are a chosen generation, a royal priesthood, a holy nation, and His own special people (see 1 Pet. 2:9). However, neither of these Scriptures has anything to do with perfection from our standpoint. Yet perfection is the image we often paint for the world to see.

DEFINING *SINNER*

Before I continue, let me define the term *sinner*, as I will be using it quite a bit throughout this book. A sinner is any man, woman, boy, or girl who possess human nature—and we all fall under that definition. It's our nature that makes us not just sinful, but sinners. We are born with the knowledge of good and evil, with the innate instinct to do evil. Not only that, but the devil often plays into those instincts, though we don't need the devil to sin and be evil; it's already within us—both the desire and ability.

Children who aren't old enough to know the difference between right and wrong and who have not been taught to do wrong (hopefully), already know how to be selfish, steal, lie, covet, hate, and so forth. It's as if the good is overpowered by the evil—and it is the great responsibility of parents to teach the good or to bring the knowledge and acts of good out in their children.

So in using the term *sinner*, I'm not necessarily just talking about liars, murderers, rapists, and those whom society and sometimes even the Church may despise. I'm also talking about people of reputable character because they still have human nature. Our nature is sinful from birth and later leads us to the acts of sin—we're sinners by nature and sinners by deeds.

Jesus taught that one must be born again—taking on the nature of God, so to speak (see John 3:1-7). This does not remove our free will, however. Adam and Eve had a nature derived from God and were in no way sinful, yet they still had free will (see Gen. 3:1-7). It was their free will (their choice of disobedience) that led them to sin, not a sinful nature that was controlling them. Therefore, born-again believers who have the indwelling power of the Holy Spirit still have free will—the choice to sin.

SAINTS STILL SIN

My sin did not disqualify me from being an heir of salvation—a saint. I am a repentant saint who committed sin. Sainthood does not eliminate the fact that we are sinful, nor does it make us immune to sin. The fact that we are sinful, however, does not mean that we are living in perpetual sin. What it does mean is that we live in a sinful world with an enemy called the devil, and we still experience human weakness and emotions stemming from our nature; we still have the propensity to sin.

Paul clearly demonstrated this when, under the inspiration of the Holy Spirit, he said, *"...Walk in the Spirit, and you shall not fulfill the lust of the flesh. For the flesh lusts against the Spirit, and the Spirit against the flesh..."* (Gal. 5:16-17). Even after we become new creations (see 2 Cor. 5:17), this is still a reality on earth—we can still sin, fulfilling fleshly lust.

Our sainthood is through the covenant relationship that we maintain in Jesus Christ. It doesn't have anything to do with how many miraculous signs or good works we've done or whether we've met the qualifications laid out by any particular church leaders or denomination. *"For by grace you have been saved through faith, and that not of yourselves; **it is the gift of God, not of works**, lest anyone should boast"* (Eph. 2:8-9).

DEEP PAIN

When my sins were staring me in the face, I wanted to give up. I really wanted to give in to hopelessness, frustration, and to simply abandon everything God had spoken about His plans for me. I was miserable; I was mad; I was upset; I was hurting deep inside! I had no idea a person could feel such deep emotional and spiritual hurt! It certainly gave me a better understanding of the pain Jesus Christ must have felt from the rejection, betrayal, denial, and ridicule He faced, having all the sins of the world placed upon Him—along with the loneliness He experienced when God the Father forsook Him.

The shame, guilt, and remorse I felt for my personal sin were unbearable! Comprehending what Jesus went through when He took the sins of the whole world upon Himself is beyond me—not to mention the fact that He was innocent. Being punished for a crime that you commit is one thing, but being punished for something that you did not do is a completely different story.

I just wanted a break from theology and Christianity. I wanted to be me—alone. If the conviction of faith and assurance in God were something physically tangible, I would have taken hold of them and thrown them aside, at least for a while. That was how I felt. At the same time, I wasn't sure what or who I'd be without my faith, without Christ in me—the hope of glory (see Col. 1:27). Fortunately, my theology and Christianity had permeated my life so much that I would first have to throw myself in the dump before I could cast it aside as if it were some dirty garment.

I recall reading and praying this psalm of David:

O LORD, do not rebuke me in Your wrath, nor chasten me in Your hot displeasure! For Your arrows pierce me deeply, and Your hand presses me down. There is no soundness in my flesh because of Your anger, nor any health in my bones because of my sin. For my iniquities have gone over my head; like a heavy burden they are too heavy for me. My wounds are foul and festering because of my foolishness. I am troubled, I am bowed down greatly; I go mourning all the day long. For my loins are full of inflammation, and there is no soundness in my flesh. I am feeble and severely broken; I groan because of the turmoil of my heart. Lord, all my desire is before You; and my sighing is not hidden from You. My heart pants, my strength fails me; as for the light of my eyes, it also has gone from me.….For I am ready to fall, and my sorrow is continually before me. For I will declare my iniquity; I will be in anguish over my sin (Psalm 38:1-18).

I struggled with the practicality and understanding of the Scriptures that I had read, memorized, and quoted so often: *"I can do all things through Christ who strengthens me"* (Phil. 4:13). *"And we know that all things work together for good to those who love God, to those who are the called according to His purpose"* (Rom. 8:28). *"Yet in all these things we are more than conquerors through Him who loved us"* (Rom. 8:37). *"No weapon formed against you shall prosper…"* (Isa. 54:17). The list went on and on.

I was faced with a situation where the scope and the reality of it were heavier than what I could lift. How could I make the words on paper that I had preached and sung about so much, which are the living Word of God, become alive to me—keeping me alive through death?

Circumstances were about to test my belief in what I preached. It is easy to tell others, "Hold on; just pray about it; God will come through; wait on the Lord; God will provide; God will make a way.…" But when you yourself are faced with the challenges of life, when you're stuck and just barely holding on for survival, then you realize it's so much easier to sing when you are on the mountaintop than when you are in the valley.

Survival was not what I was looking for, however. I wanted my life and my story to bring glory to God. I knew the Lord had called me and that He had a wonderful plan for my life. But I hadn't seen this coming. In my head, I had a picture of the landing of my destiny, and it was beautiful, but I had no foreknowledge that I would fall into such a big pothole of sin on the journey.

The challenges I found myself in, and the ones that were awaiting me, were insurmountable! I was in jail. I now had a reproachable criminal record. I was no longer a worship team member. I was no longer a part of the Bible college community. I was no longer a candidate for any ministry opportunity. From what I understood, nobody wanted me to come and preach in their church anymore. It seemed like all my dreams, my very destiny, had fallen apart.

But thank God for a wonderful minister friend named Pastor Len, from Medicine Hat, Alberta, who came to visit me a few times to let me know that he loves me, cares about me, and will help me. He also brought numerous books for me to read, in addition to the ones my wife and mother-in-law sent me. Sometimes that's all you need—someone to remind you of the promises of God and to let you know you can lean on them.

It would have been a much greater encouragement if that kind of hopeful, restoring love had come from the church community, but it didn't. Sometimes we'll support and seek the restoration of others, but it's only when the sin or damage is controlled and confined—then we can still maintain our image to a degree. But should the sin or damage become public knowledge and grow beyond our ability to control or minimize its effect, then rejection often replaces such support. This is especially true for those who have had similar sinful falls in the past. Certainly this was my experience. Nonetheless, I'm still reaching out to my brethren for their forgiveness because I am truly repentant.

THE JOURNEY

What I've come to learn is that when the Lord calls you to a purpose and plan, He doesn't usually reveal all the details of how that plan will unfold. He commissions you to begin your journey (like Abraham, see Gen. 12:1-3); He gives you a picture of the purpose and destination, but He doesn't necessarily tell you about the journey itself—what challenges you must face, endure, and overcome.

If the Lord had told Joseph the things he would have to go through in order to be positioned so he could accomplish God's plan for his life, I'm not sure he would have said, "Yes, Lord, to Your will and Your way," or "Send me, send me, please!" Speaking of Joseph, the Book of Psalms says, *"Until the time that his word came to pass, the word of the LORD tested him"* (Ps. 105:19). It's easy to embrace the great and victorious testimony of others and to admire their glory, but it's not so easy to embrace the testing they've had to go through or the sometimes difficult and ugly stories behind their glory.

Now one might ask, "Was it God's plan and will for Joseph to be treated so wickedly by his brothers and then to be framed and thrown in prison?" I don't think so. God does not orchestrate evil, though He allows the orchestrating of evil. But He is still able to bring about His good will through it. What I do know is that God sees the whole picture and works all things out according to the counsel of His will (see Eph. 1:11). Joseph himself said to his brothers, *"...you meant evil against me; but God meant it for good, in order to bring it about as it is this day, to save many people alive"* (Gen. 50:20).

We are not informed about all the specifics of the journey because it must be traveled by faith. What we are assured of, thankfully, is a safe landing and the arrival at our destination. No one can pluck us out of His hand. But we can walk away through rebellion and disobedience onto the road of apostasy. *"Let us therefore be diligent to enter that rest, lest anyone fall according to the same example of disobedience"* (Heb. 4:11).

ONCE SAVED, ALWAYS SAVED?

Do I believe in "once saved, always saved"? I do, but only for those who remain in the covenant relationship. It's not surprising that some would teach this "once saved, always saved" doctrine from any standpoint; some even believe the devil will eventually be saved. In such a case, it would be no big deal to keep on living in the pleasures of sin and be like the devil himself. The thinking may go, *If he's going to be saved and he's the father of all evil, then we should all be just fine—right?* Not so fast. Not all the Israelites who left Egypt entered the Promised Land. Rather, God declared to them (as He declares now to us), *"You shall be holy, for I the LORD your God am holy"* (Lev. 19:2) and *"Pursue...holiness, without which no one will see the Lord"* (Heb. 12:14).

The Bible does not endorse anyone coming to Christ for initial salvation and then returning to the unfruitful works of darkness. Nowhere does it say that they will still be saved if they don't repent and renounce such a lifestyle. I'm aware that some may argue about the legitimacy of the initial salvation experience of those who fall away—like Judas, for example. However, the parable of the sower indicates otherwise. One group of seeds fell on thorny soil, and they were choked out by the cares of this world and the deceitfulness of riches. Though they fell away, Jesus did not give any indication that they hadn't received the word (salvation) with a sincere heart (see Matt. 13).

In addition to this, Paul mentioned those who had *strayed* from the faith because of their greediness and love for money and who had pierced themselves through with many sorrows (see 1 Tim. 6:10). Paul asserted that at one point some were on the right path, but they eventually strayed. (See also Second Thessalonians 2:3, which tells about the great falling away.)

> *Jesus said, "Enter by the narrow gate; for wide is the gate and broad is the way that leads to destruction, and there are many who go in by it. Because narrow is the gate and difficult is the way which leads to life, and there are few who find it"* (Matthew 7:13-14).

None of us saints really knows what we will or will not encounter on the narrow road that leads to life eternal. Fortunately, though, if we continue on that road with a true heart, the destination is inevitable.

Paul was one of the few saints who was given an insight about what his journey ahead would entail (see Acts 9:1-16). But regardless of the fact that Paul was told he would suffer many things for the sake of Christ and the fact that he was ready to die for the cross, even then, he wasn't given a detailed description of what he would have to go through.

Though the things he experienced on his journey were not because of a sinful nature, brought about by his own doing, they're still noteworthy because some of them were painful enough that they could have caused him to give up rather than continue on.

Here is what Paul said about his experience and credentials:

> *Are they Hebrews? So am I. Are they Israelites? So am I. Are they the seed of Abraham? So am I. Are they the ministers of Christ?—I speak as a fool—I am more: in labors more abundant, in stripes above measure, in prisons more frequently, in deaths often. From the Jews five times I received forty stripes minus one. Three times I was beaten with rods; once I was*

*stoned; three times I was shipwrecked; a night and a day I
have been in the deep; in journeys often, in perils of waters,
in perils of robbers, in perils of my own countrymen, in per-
ils of the Gentiles, in perils in the city, in perils in the wilderness, in perils in the sea, in perils among false brethren,
in weariness and toil, in sleeplessness often, in hunger and
thirst, in fasting often, in cold and nakedness—besides the
other things, what comes upon me daily: my deep concern
for all the churches. Who is weak, and I am not weak? Who
is made to stumble, and I do not burn with indignation?*
(2 Corinthians 11:22-29)

On my journey, I've experienced some hardship and pain that
resulted from my own sinful acts; at other times, the struggle was
not a result of my actions. If I had known that I would end up in
jail with a despicable criminal record, I would not have gone to
Bible college when the Lord told me to go, even though my most
terrible fall came after I had completed my studies. I would have
rebelled. But the good plan and the good work had already been
set in motion by Almighty God, and He will perfectly accomplish
what He has started in me.

RESTORE SUCH A ONE

Though with humility I seek the forgiveness of my victim,
the Church, and even society; I also believe I must address some
issues of deep concern within the Church. My experience has
given me great insight into these issues.

It was a heartbreaking time of my life! I could not find words
to express myself. And even if I did find the words, I was overwhelmed with emotion and tears; I could not speak clearly! But
deep down in my heart, even though I was an outcast from the

Church community, I knew I was still a saint, still a child of God, and still loved by God.

It was a difficult time to say the least. I prayed; I cried; I groaned! I realized that, though I had fallen in sin disgracefully, the community of saints that I was a part of, except for a few, had also sinned by omission. Galatians 6:1-2 says,

Brethren, if a man is overtaken in any trespass, you who are spiritual restore such a one in a spirit of gentleness, considering yourself lest you also be tempted. Bear one another's burdens, and so fulfill the law of Christ.

This Scripture is a command. We are called to help restore those who have fallen—leading them to full repentance and helping them find total healing so that they are free to pursue their destiny in Christ. I didn't research the restoration process of evangelist Jimmy Swaggart, but it's sure graceful to see him back on the journey of faith for the Lord. Spiritual maturity is not a result of merely praying three times a day, reading the Bible through once every year, memorizing and quoting Scriptures, or being faithful in personal devotions, though these have their proper place in believers' lives. Maturity has more to do with doing what the Word says—being Spirit-led and ministering life where there is death, hope where there is hopelessness. It is a way of life that operates out of God's love and grace and not out of concern for personal interests, motives, and image.

We are commanded to help each other when we fall, and when someone falls, we should consider ourselves lest we also are tempted. In other words, it could've been any one of us. But instead of helping the fallen saints, many of us look down on our brothers and sisters with a sense of bewilderment, saying things like, "How could they do that?" or "They weren't living right; otherwise, they wouldn't have done that." But are we forgetting that Moses was living right during the time when He disobeyed God by striking the rock twice and sinning in his anger (see Num. 20:7-13). David also was living right before he fell into his famous sin (see 2 Sam. 9–11).

Some believers even take pride in the fact that others have fallen. Instead of reacting with compassion, they use the mistakes of others to make themselves feel "holier" and more "sanctified." But such an attitude is so far from true Christianity and the heart of God. It's not surprising when the world refuses to forgive, especially those who have committed terrible crimes like I have. But the Church is called to a different standard. We are called to love the unlovable, to fight for the lost and broken, and to heal our fallen brethren, even when the sin is ugly and gross.

It's easy to focus on the obvious sinful actions of others and fail to realize that sometimes we too sin in the way we respond or fail to respond. Even as I have considered these things, I have also been challenged that I cannot be unmerciful and unforgiving toward those who reacted wrongly to me. After all, if the tides were turned and it was someone else who did what I did, maybe I would've responded the same way—it's possible. But my experience of falling into sin and being rejected because of it has taught me a great deal, and I do not believe my future response toward others could be anything but graceful, incorporated with righteous justice.

I'm not on a mission to knock the Church community for the sin of omission. Rather, I want to remind believers of the Word of God regarding certain issues—sin, sinners, saints, forgiveness, church discipline, restoration, and so forth. My heart's cry is that we would learn to follow through in obedience even when it hurts and may put our reputations and images on the line. Restoration and forgiveness, for example, should not be something we do when we feel like it, but something we do because we represent the heart of God.

A HIGHER STANDARD

The Church is called to operate from a higher standard than the world, though many times we fall short. We are commanded to love those who are our enemies, to do good to those who hate us, to bless those who curse us, to pray for those who spitefully use us, to repay with good those who do evil to us, and to forgive those who sin against us (see Matt. 5:43-46; Luke 6:37-38; Rom. 12:17).

If we know that others have an issue with us, we're commanded to take the initiative to go to them and make it right (see Matt. 18:15-17). If we're honest, we'll admit that sometimes we love, bless, do good to others, and forgive not because we want to or delight in doing it, but because we're commanded to. Not only that, but we know that ignoring God's commands also means that we'd be hurting ourselves and tying God's hands (so to speak) concerning His blessings over our lives.

Furthermore, Jesus said,

...If you forgive men their trespasses, your heavenly Father will also forgive you. But if you do not forgive men their trespasses, neither will your Father forgive your trespasses (Matthew 6:14-15).

Job, when he was talking with his friends, said,

To him who is afflicted, kindness should be shown by his friend, even though he forsakes the fear of the Almighty. My

*brothers have dealt deceitfully like a brook, like the streams of
the brooks that pass away* (Job 6:14-15).

I had not turned my back on the Lord, but I was and still am
committed to serving Him. I thought that would have been at
least an underlying factor in the saints seeking my correction and
restoration, but it didn't happen.

PUNISHMENT AND HOPE

I knew God loved me even though He was punishing me for
my sins. He was disappointed with me, but His disappointment
and punishment were just. Hebrews 12:4-7 says,

*You have not yet resisted to bloodshed, striving against sin.
And you have forgotten the exhortation which speaks to you as
to sons: "My son, do not despise the chastening of the LORD,
nor be discouraged when you are rebuked by Him; for whom
the LORD loves He chastens, and scourges every son whom He
receives." If you endure chastening, God deals with you as with
sons; for what son is there whom a father does not chasten?*

My only hope was the Word of God and His promises to
me. When I couldn't see His hand, I had to trust His plan. What
I couldn't see, I had to trust Him for by faith. When I couldn't
understand, I had to ask Him to hold my hand.

The devil was trying to overwhelm me with feelings of
guilt, shame, embarrassment, worthlessness, condemnation, and
hopelessness—the thought that it was all over. "God won't forgive
you for this terrible sinful act. Your reputation is ruined, and God
is angry with you because you've brought reproach to His name,"
he said, seeking to poison my mind. But the Lord was with me
and would not let him conquer me.

I was able to distinguish the conviction of the Holy Spirit from the condemnation coming from the devil. God's conviction, discipline, and rebuke always point to a solution, a way of making things right, and the hopeful expectation of being forgiven and restored.

When the Lord convicts us, it is with the hope that we will not stay where we are, but that we will repent. The condemnation of the devil, however, gives no light at the end of the tunnel. It leaves us in the pit of shame, guilt, oppression, depression, and unworthiness—with the case closed! This is one of the main reasons why many people commit suicide—whether it has to do with their self-esteem, something they have done, or a situation they find themselves in. The devil's repetitious sermon to them is, "That's the way things are, and that's the way they will be. No one cares; no one loves you; and no one will even miss you." He doesn't give hope; he gives hopelessness.

Through the power of the Holy Spirit, the Lord caused me to remember His written and spoken Word. He said, *"If we confess our sins, He is faithful and just to forgive us our sins and to cleanse us from all unrighteousness"* (1 John 1:9), and *"The sacrifices of God are a broken spirit, a broken and a contrite heart—these, O God You will not despise"* (Ps. 51:17). I was reminded of many great servants and prophets of God, saints who had sinned disgracefully, but were forgiven, called, and used mightily of God in spite of their flaws.

From then on, I began taking more courage. I said to myself, "If the Lord called David, knowing that he was going to sin, and forgave him when he did, then He will forgive me too. If He pardoned Moses and used him, He can do the same for me. If He called Peter and told him of his future denial, but still chose him, prayed for him, forgave him, and used him, then God can do the same for me."

My very first night in jail, the Lord assured me of His sovereignty, omniscience, and omnipotence. He reminded me of His prophetic words that had been spoken over my life on many different occasions and in different forms.

THE BATTLE FOR MY LIFE

Shortly before everything fell apart, one Sunday morning I was at the church altar praying. Then I saw in my spirit a man with whom I was familiar coming up to place his hand on me and to pray for me. Less than a minute after I had the vision, I felt a hand resting on my shoulder, and the person started praying for me. And of course, it was the person I had seen in my vision. After he was finished praying for me, he told me to stand up and look at him. Then he said to me, "There is a great spiritual battle going on over your life because the devil wants to stop what God has planned for you."

I knew the Lord had (and still has) a great plan for my life. But I became aware more than ever before that spiritual warfare was heating up over my life! Obviously, satan is always at work to stop or even delay the work of God in our lives. I didn't know what to anticipate, but I knew my life was in God's hands. And in that I took comfort. I knew there were areas in my life that needed to die. It was sin—strongholds—bondage! I wanted to change and let them go, but it seemed as if they were determined not to let me go.

While the heavens were waging war on my behalf, I was fighting one of my own—internally! I didn't cry out to God for help like I should have. Neither did I put in place boundaries and disciplines to protect myself. Yet in His grace, God gave me many dreams that were all related in some way—telling me that the devil was coming after me in full force (to sift me out, so to speak), that I would experience tremendous pain and setback, but that I would not end as a prey of the enemy who seeks to steal, kill, and destroy, but as a victor over him.

The grace of God in these dreams was His loving concern for me. He promised that, if I would seek Him and change my sinful ways, the content of the dreams wouldn't come to pass. I did not respond properly to my situation or to the many examples in the Old Testament where God persistently warned His people to seek Him and turn from their wicked ways in order to avoid looming destruction (see Jer. 3–4; 25:1-14; Isa. 30; 27:9-15; 9:8-17; Amos 5:1-15; Zeph. 2:1-3).

I never saw myself in jail, let alone hurting someone the way I did. But that's exactly what happened. O how my heart hurts just knowing how deeply I've hurt someone! Though I'm still deal-ing with painful consequences as the victimizer, the victim of my deplorable crime must be suffering much, much more from the scars and trauma of my actions! I deserve the consequences that I'm dealing with from the justice system. It was my own making and foolishness that caused me to become criminal in behavior. But the victim is dealing with hurts that nobody would choose to go through. The trauma was not invited; it was inflicted.

How do family members live with a relative who has been crippled to the point of being a "vegetable"? How do they view the drunk driver who crashed into their car or house, inflicting the damage? That's tough to deal with even if you're a theologian and Bible scholar! Though my crimes were of a different nature, and I was not drunk, I acknowledge with deep regret that I caused

enormous, psychologically-crippling wounds and scars to someone who was a friend.

OTHER SAINTS WHO SINNED

As I mentioned previously, many Bible heroes committed
awful sins, even while walking with the Lord. Yet God forgave
and redeemed them from their bad choices. He did not remove
their destiny or calling, but healed them and enabled them to do
great things for Him.

In the next few chapters I want to examine the stories of some
of these men and women of faith in an unconventional way. It's
easy to read Bible stories without relating to the personal elements
behind the events—the emotions and thoughts of the people who
actually lived those stories. The Bible omits many details, and
much of the character's narratives in these chapters is conjecture.
Still, I believe reading between the lines of their stories will give
us valuable insight and help us to relate to their humanity—to
remember that we are all capable, apart from the grace of God, of
committing the worst sins.

CHAPTER 2

DAVID'S STORY

Anybody Is Capable of Anything

 The heart is deceitful above all things, and desperately wicked... (Jeremiah 17:9).

Many people are familiar with the unbelievable victory that I, David, won over the giant, Goliath (see 1 Sam. 17). Some know me as the little shepherd boy; some know me as King Solomon's father; some know me as a king of Israel; some know me as a skilled musician—writer of psalms and songs; and some know me as the man after God's own heart (see 1 Sam. 13:13-14). But not too many know me as the saint who sinned by committing adultery and murder—to name a few of my sins (see 2 Sam. 11).

I was just a little shepherd boy in Israel taking care of my father's flock. In the quietness of the fields—the cloudy, cold, and rainy days; the beautiful sunrises and sunsets; the bright moonlight and starry skies; the brushing of the breeze on my skin; the wonder of nature and all its abundant life forms—I became a worshiper and a skilled player on the harp. I used to admire the heavens above and be amazed with the awesomeness of God, my Creator.

These were the experiences that really gave birth to many of my psalms, such as Psalm 19.

> *The heavens declare the glory of God; and the firmament shows His handiwork. Day unto day utters speech, and night unto night reveals knowledge. There is no speech nor language where their voice is not heard. Their line has gone out through all the earth, and their words to the end of the world...* (Psalm 19:1-4).

Some days I longed to be home in the comfort of my house, but on the other hand, I knew I was drawing closer to the God of my fathers, the God of Abraham, Isaac, and Jacob. I wanted to know Him personally so I could call Him "my God." And being in the fields away from the fast-paced life provided a great opportunity for just that.

Sometimes though, it was challenging because I would have to face death in the eye, taking on lions and bears that sought to devour my sheep and my own life. Without hesitation, I would go after that bear or lion, strike it, and rescue my sheep. Then, if it turned on me, I would overcome it and kill it. Thus was my life as the little shepherd boy until the Lord placed His mighty hand upon me and began to usher me into His purpose.

Promotion

My love for the Lord was steadfast. I loved Him with all my heart, with all my soul, and with all my strength! I was anointed to be king of Israel by Samuel, the prophet (see 1 Sam. 16:1-13), but I did not ascend to the kingdom until many years later. Eventually I was summoned to the reigning king, King Saul, to sooth his spirit by playing my harp for him because he was being oppressed by an evil spirit (see 1 Sam. 16:14-23). I played to the best of my ability, and the Lord granted His anointing through my music, causing the evil spirit to flee from Saul.

One day I went to visit my brothers who were soldiers in the field; there I saw the Philistine army and their champion, Goliath, taunting and reproaching the people of Israel! I became angry in defense of the name of my God! Being fully aware of the awesome power and mighty hand of God, who brought His people out of bondage in Egypt, I was convinced He would give me the power to defeat this "uncircumcised" Philistine for the glory of His name. And He did.

King Saul did not want me to fight Goliath because I was only a teenager, not an experienced warrior. But I kept insisting on my abilities in confronting danger. Plus, I argued, God was with me. So Saul gave in to my pressure and gave me his very own armor to put on, but it was too big and heavy. It was not my thing. I told him I'd use what God had given me and gifted me in.

So I took my slingshot and got five smooth stones and went to face Goliath head on. I didn't have to fire a second time. The first stone hit him, and he fell. Then I ran over to him, took his own sword, and cut off his head (see 1 Sam. 17:48-51).

So there I was, becoming all that God wanted me to be. The journey wasn't easy, though. I spent years in the wilderness running from King Saul, who had decided he hated me and was trying to kill me. Eventually, the Lord did bring me into the kingdom He'd promised me, and He enabled me to have many great victories in battle.

MY BLIND SPOT

I was walking in my integrity and praying according to the uprightness of my heart. If anyone were to ask me, "Do you ever see yourself committing adultery?" I would have said, "Absolutely not! God forbid!" If they were to ask me, "Do you see yourself ever committing murder, coldblooded murder at that?" I would have most definitely said, "No way. I'm a man of integrity, and I love the precepts and laws of God more than my own food! I would not sin against the Lord by doing that."

The truth is, and many of you already know it, that the very acts that I preached against I was not far from committing myself. I was so focused on the shortcomings in others that I failed to recognize my own weaknesses. I even remember praying prayers like this one: *"The LORD rewarded me according to my righteousness; according to the cleanness of my hands He has recompensed me"* (Ps. 18:20).

Eventually, the time came when I should've been at war, for it was the time when kings go out to war, but I stayed home. I wanted just to relax—to take it easy. After all, I had accomplished much. But I was just like my fathers who, after they had conquered much of the Promised Land, became complacent and failed to drive out the inhabitants completely and possess the entire land.

MY FALL

One day as I was walking on the roof of my house, I looked and saw a beautiful woman, Bathsheba, bathing. I sent to inquire about her and was told that she was the wife of Uriah, the Hittite. Nonetheless, I had her brought to my palace and slept with her, then sent her back home (see 2 Sam. 11:2-5).

The underlining truth in this is that when you take your eyes off the promise and the purpose, all you will see is your own self-satisfaction. She was someone else's wife; she was the helpmate to another man. Even though she was already taken, I still took her. And no, she didn't necessarily come of her own free will. My servants brought her; she didn't have much of a choice. I was king. Don't think that because I was the king all the women wanted to sleep with me or be my wife. Yes, there were many who would've loved to be my wife at a moment's notice; I know that. But she was already married to an exceptional man—one of my mighty men.

Disgrace was about to cover my face. I had committed adultery, and after learning that the woman had become pregnant, I devised a plan to cover up my sin. I brought her husband, Uriah, home from war in the hopes that he would make love to her. Then it would seem as if the child was his. But that didn't work. He refused to go home to his wife to indulge in pleasure while his comrades were still on the battlefield; this he did even though I had commanded him to go home and take a break.

After he refused to go home, I told Uriah to stick around till the next day. For the remainder of that day and all night long, I went back and forth about what to do next. The following day I brought him into the palace and made him drink so much wine that he became drunk, hoping that he would then set aside his principles and integrity and go home to his wife—but that didn't work either. He went and slept where the other servants slept.

So I pondered again, all night, over my next move. If those behaviors weren't vicious and cruel enough, early the next morning I gave him his own execution letter to take to the commander of the army. In the letter, I told the commander to put Uriah on the frontline of the hottest battle and then retreat from him so he would be struck down. The plan was executed exactly the way I planned it. Unfortunately, my inconsiderate, sinful heart not only led to the death of Uriah, but it also caused the death of some of my greatest warriors who were on the frontline with him (see 2 Sam. 11:14-24).

It's hard to believe that I, the king of Israel and a worshiper of God, would do such awful things. But I didn't stop there. I was so foolish. Did I do all that with the belief that God didn't see? Or was I naïve enough to think that God sees all things, but He would not address my sins? I tried to pretend like nothing had happened, but it was too late.

CONFRONTED BY THE PROPHET

As a true worshiper of God, when I sinned, the peace of God in my heart was affected. In my spirit there was war, but it wasn't intense enough that it caused me to budge—at least not yet. Slowly, but surely, the grip of unconfessed sin began to take its toll on me.

When I kept silent, my bones grew old through my groaning all the day long. For day and night Your hand was heavy upon me; my vitality was turned into the drought of summer. I acknowledged my sin to You, and my iniquity I have not

*hidden. I said, "I will confess my transgressions to the LORD,"
and You forgave the iniquity of my sin* (Psalm 32:3-5).

Unfortunately, it was not until the Lord sent His servant
Nathan to me that I escaped and made things right. I was living in the sin of unrepentance for months; once the child whom
I fathered with Bathsheba was born I was forced to deal with
the sin in my life. The man of God came and confronted me.
Nathan described my own sin to me in the form of a parable that
demanded a judgment call from the king.

He spoke of a rich man who had many flocks and herds and
a poor man who had nothing—except one little ewe lamb. The
poor man had bought the lamb, nourished it, and raised it with
his children. It drank from his cup and was like a daughter to him.

Then a wayfaring traveler came to the rich man for help, but
the rich man refused to take from his own flock or herd to prepare
meat and food for the wary traveler. Instead, he went to the poor
man, took away his only ewe lamb that was so precious to him,
prepared it, and offered it to the traveler.

When the prophet Nathan told me this parable, it bothered
me so much. I became outraged at the rich man for his thought-
less and unjust acts toward the poor man! I thought to myself, *This
man has no fear of Almighty God. Such a man should not dwell in this
land. He deserves to die!*

These are the exact words recorded in Second Samuel 12:5-6:

*So David's anger was greatly aroused against the man, and
he said to Nathan, "As the LORD lives, the man who has
done this shall surely die! And he shall restore fourfold for the
lamb, because he did this thing and because he had no pity."*

As soon as I expressed my utmost displeasure toward the rich man, Nathan said to me, "You are the man." Ouch! Then he went on to say how the Lord had anointed me king, delivered me from King Saul, given me my master's house and many wives—and if that wasn't enough, He would still have given me more. But I had despised the Lord by killing Uriah and taking his wife to be my wife. This was unbelievable! I had sworn by the Lord that the man who had done such acts would *surely die*—not knowing that I was the man.

Though I myself was guilty of such double-standard hypocrisy, I confessed and repented bitterly, saying,

Have mercy on me, O God, according to Your lovingkindness; according to the multitude of Your tender mercies, blot out my transgressions. Wash me thoroughly from my iniquity, and cleanse me from my sin. For I acknowledge my transgressions, and my sin is always before me. Against You, You only, have I sinned, and done this evil in Your sight—that You may be found just when You speak, and blameless when You judge. Behold, I was brought forth in iniquity, and in sin my mother conceived me. Behold, You desire truth in the inward parts, and in the hidden part You will make me to know wisdom. Purge me with hyssop, and I shall be clean; wash me, and I shall be whiter than snow. Make me hear joy and gladness, that the bones You have broken may rejoice. Hide Your face from my sins, and blot out all my iniquities. Create in me a clean heart, O God, and renew a steadfast spirit within me. Do not cast me away from Your presence, and do not take Your Holy Spirit from me. Restore to me the joy of Your salvation, and uphold me by Your generous Spirit. Then I will teach transgressors Your ways, and sinners shall be converted to You. Deliver me from the guilt of bloodshed, O

God, the God of my salvation, and my tongue shall sing aloud of Your righteousness. O Lord, open my lips, and my mouth shall show forth Your praise. For You do not desire sacrifice, or else I would give it; You do not delight in burnt offering. The sacrifices of God are a broken spirit, a broken and a contrite heart—these, O God, You will not despise (Psalm 51:1-17).

My sin with Bathsheba was a warm-blooded sin—pretty much in the heat of the moment. It was not something I was planning for weeks or days; nor was I stalking her in the past and lusting after her. I had let my guard down and was not about the Lord's business—I was being idle. I arose from my bed in the evening. That's when I saw Bathsheba bathing and was tempted. It was early in the evening when one would normally be slowly getting ready for bed, not getting out of bed.

I had been sleeping most of the afternoon. I was tempted and was not on guard to resist—not because I was sleeping in the afternoon, but because my heart and mind were not where they should've been.

The murder of Uriah was a cold-blooded sin. The process that led up to the murder took days. After trying to cover up my sin with failed attempts, I then sat up all night pondering what to do next. I was blinded by my initial sin and thus deceitfully planned his murder. All I could think about was self-preservation.

I began to realize I wasn't much different from Adam and Eve who, when they had sinned, tried to shift the blame to others to avoid taking responsibility (see Gen. 3:6-13). They were willing to cover up their sin by any means and at any cost. I was willing to let many of my greatest warriors die just so one man would die and thereby put an end to my sin spiral.

I repented of my sins, but there were still consequences I had to deal with. My son born to Bathsheba got sick and died a few days later (see 2 Sam. 12:15-18). But the Lord redeemed my relationship with Bathsheba. She bore me another son, Solomon, who would succeed me as king. Soon after his birth, the Lord sent word through Nathan to name him Jedidiah, which means beloved of the Lord (see 2 Sam. 12:24-25).

I've had many experiences of joy and tears, ups and downs. Through all my pain, fear, tears, shame, even sin, the Lord was still with me. Though I acknowledge that I wasn't perfect, when I fell in sin I trusted the Lord for His perfect and complete forgiveness. One thing I can say about myself—I didn't take sin lightly! Whenever I fell, I was always in anguish over my sins. Thus many of my bitter prayers of repentance and seeking God's grace are recorded in the Book of Psalms.

RAY'S REFLECTIONS AND INSIGHTS

David's story has been a great encouragement to me, and I have seen many parallels in it with my own life. For example, like David, I never planned to commit such an awful crime. It's a good reminder to all of us that even though we may never see ourselves planning to do certain things, we must pray that God would keep us back from all sins because we truly don't know what we're capable of. We often fail to see God's grace at work, keeping and protecting us from certain situations and sins. At times His grace will sustain and ultimately deliver us through the "fire" (as He has done with me), but it can also keep us from experiencing the "fire" in the first place.

Jeremiah, speaking for the Lord, said,

The heart is deceitful above all things, and desperately wicked; who can know it? I, the LORD, search the heart, I test the mind, even to give every man according to his ways, according to the fruit of his doings (Jeremiah 17:9-10).

Even the apostle Peter, who said he would never deny Jesus, but that he would go all the way with Him, even to death, ended up denying the Messiah (see Luke 22:31-34). But we will discuss that more later.

Like David, I found myself doing something I never imagined possible, in large part because I was not guarding my heart and being diligent to pursue God's calling in my life. David stayed home when he should have been in battle, and I too "stayed home" from the spiritual battle in my life. When we're not at work, about the Father's business, we're likely to fall into the trap of being idle or about someone else's business, even our own. Here are some words of wisdom: we must make sure that we are where we're supposed to be and that we are doing what we're supposed to be doing.

The words of the apostle Peter could not have made it any clearer: *"Be sober, be vigilant; because your adversary the devil walks about like a roaring lion, seeking whom he may devour. Resist him, steadfast in the faith..."* (1 Pet. 5:8-9). When we do not submit ourselves to the Lord, we are incapable of resisting the *"...lust of the flesh, the lust of the eyes, and the pride of life..."* (1 John 2:16), and the devil often presents them to us at the opportune time of weakness, when we've taken our eyes off of the Lord.

DAVID REMAINED KING

One of the most striking elements of David's story is that he remained king even after his sins. Though God had removed the king before him, Saul, for his pride, disobedience, and refusal to repent (see 1 Sam. 13:1-14), He did not remove David from the throne. God wanted to show that David's position in Him was not based on his status as a king or on his ability to be a perfect king. David wasn't perfect, but he repented wholeheartedly when he sinned, and that made all the difference, especially in comparison to King Saul.

Typically the Church is very quick to remove someone from leadership or ministry the second they fall into sin. But God didn't do it to David even though his sins were much worse than what most Christians commit. Certainly, the Church has freedom and responsibility to administer discipline, but more often than not, discipline is taken overboard while helping and restoring is neglected.

If God wanted David to get things right and remain in his ministry as the king, but the leadership under him and the rest of the people insisted that he be removed, then they would have been opposing God's purpose. If God forgives a person, but people refuse to, they are essentially saying they're greater than God and have the power and authority to veto His decree. When God says "yes" and we say "no," we set out to oppose God. Even though we may think we get our way, ultimately we'll never win.

After I fell into sin, some leaders and pastors didn't want anything to do with me; some of them even encouraged my wife to leave me. If the son of one of those leaders had done what I did, or committed a crime of a different nature, the leader would still love and support his child—while making his disappointment and utmost disapproval of the behavior clear. More than likely, he would do it even in opposition to the will of his church. And should he have to choose between his son and his ministry position in the church, he maybe would still choose his son. But I was not a son, so I received different treatment. Fortunately, I have a heavenly Father who, even if my mother and father forsake me, will take care of me and redeem me as His purchased possession (see Ps. 27:10; 1 Cor. 6:20).

As much as I am seeking the Church's forgiveness, I cannot hinge my salvation on it; even if my brothers and sisters do not forgive me, I will not abandon my faith. My salvation is centered on Jesus Christ and His ability and willingness to forgive me when I fall short, to justify me in His righteousness. I must press on regardless.

I've seen what has happened to Jimmy Swaggart, Jim Bakker, Ted Haggard, and many other men and women of God, known and not so well-known, who fell into sin. When they fell, some of the saints seem to write them off as if God cannot correct, pardon, change, and restore them.

Some of us are more messed up than others, but we have all had to deal with some sort of "sin mess" in our lives. The world knows that we're not as perfect as many within the Church community would claim, at least from a human point of view. It's when we try to proclaim that we haven't messed up or give the impression that we're not capable of messing up—and then we do—that we really look like hypocrites.

When David said in Psalm 119:11, *"Your word I have hidden in my heart, that I might not sin against You,"* he wasn't saying that doing so makes it impossible for us to sin. That could not have been the case because he did sin more than once. Putting God's Word in our hearts does make it harder for us to sin. But we still have God-given free will; we can choose to obey or not.

The Word of God is there to help us counteract temptation to sin, enabling us to speak the truth of God's Word, arrest every lying thought, and take them captive to the obedience of Christ (see 2 Cor. 10:3-6). Without the law, for example, sin was not imputed, because people did not know their "right hand from their left." But when the law (the Word) was given, sin could be clearly seen, and people were admonished and commanded to abstain from sin. What did Jesus use to counteract and overcome the temptations of the devil? It was the Word, written and hidden in His heart. In Psalm 119 David wrote, *"Your word is a lamp to my feet and a light to my path"* (Ps. 119:105). Is it all making sense now?

HISTORY REPEATED

Another element of David's story that strikes home with me is the irony of his judgment toward the rich man. Many saints are "killing" their fellow brothers and sisters for acts that they themselves are doing.

The apostle Paul, in one of his writings, said,

You, therefore, who teach another, do you not teach yourself? You who preach that a man should not steal, do you steal? You who say, "Do not commit adultery," do you commit adultery? You who abhor idols, do you rob temples? You who make your boast in the law, do you dishonor God through breaking the law? For "the name of God is blasphemed among the Gentiles because of you," as it is written (Romans 2:21-24).

David wanted to kill the man whom the prophet Nathan described to him, but when he understood that the person he was so quick to kill was himself, he was shattered and wept deeply! We must be careful of the words we speak to and about others. Let them be sweet—seasoned with grace—because we may find ourselves having to turn around and eat them. David had to eat his.

We must be careful not to judge—that is, judgment based on motives and appearance as opposed to righteous judgments (see John 7:21-24). David certainly shows us that anyone, even the greatest lover of God, is capable of anything. His story does not just include how he slew Goliath; it also includes embarrassing moments of sin, weakness, and stumbling setbacks! Anybody is capable of anything. We can go from being murderers in our hearts by hating our brother (according to First John 3:15), to an attempted murderer, to a convicted murderer, all the way to a serial killer, and ultimately to a full-blown mass murderer. Each one will have to answer to God.

God does not take pleasure in the death of the wicked, but desires that they would turn from their wicked ways (see Ezek. 18:23). How much more, then, does He desire that when righteous saints fall, they be restored? When David committed adultery, it was a physical sin and obvious to all because his sin found him out. The same was true for me. I could not hide what I had done.

But too often those who secretly go around fantasizing in their hearts about their own "Bathsheba" or "David" would condemn to the grave the person who is found guilty of the physical act. The brother who does in his heart what David did physically is no less guilty and, therefore, no more righteous. The brother who does in his heart what Moses did to the Egyptian who was beating his fellow Hebrew is no less guilty and, therefore, no more righteous (see Exod. 2:11-15).

PASSING JUDGMENT

When it comes to casting judgment, it seems as if we have forgotten the prudent words of Paul: *"Therefore let him who thinks he stands take heed lest he fall"* (1 Cor. 10:12). David's relationship with God was much closer than many, if not all, of us, yet he fell into such great sin. It's discomforting how quickly we condemn each other when, in fact, we all are capable of the same things and more. David's son, King Solomon wrote, *"He who trusts in his own heart is a fool, but whoever walks wisely will be delivered"* (Prov. 28:26).

Paul declared in Galatians 2:21, *"I do not set aside the grace of God; for if righteousness* [being a saint] *comes through* [observing] *the law, then Christ died in vain."*

DISCIPLINE

Saints who sin are in no way free of some sort of disciplinary consequence, whether directly or indirectly, from God. If they haven't completely fallen into unrepentant apostasy, they remain in their position as saints. The enforcement of this disciplinary action is not exclusively left up to the Church, although the Church does have biblical grounds on which to administer it.

The Lord is sovereign in the timing, methods, and avenues through which He brings discipline. Many churches have written in their own constitution when and how disciplinary action is to be taken. But a close look at the New Testament writings will reveal more—a balanced admonishment for the Church to help and restore fallen saints (see Gal. 6:1-2; James 2:8-13; 5:19-20; Jude 20-23; Rev. 2:1-7; 2 Cor. 2:1-9; 2 Tim. 2:20-22; 1 Pet. 4:7-11). In judgment, we must never forget to show love and mercy. We may find ourselves in need of it one day.

Paul, under the inspiration of the Holy Spirit, had a lot to say about correction and discipline among believers, especially when dealing with an immoral brother. But he also had this to say:

> *...If anyone has caused grief, he has not grieved me, but all of you to some extent—not to be too severe. This punishment which was inflicted by the majority is sufficient for such a man, so that, on the contrary, you ought rather to forgive and comfort him, lest perhaps such a one be swallowed up with too much sorrow. Therefore I urge you to reaffirm your love to him. For to this end I also wrote, that I might put you to the test, whether you are obedient in all things* (2 Corinthians 2:5-9).

I've experienced firsthand what Paul was talking about. There were days when my sorrow was beyond what I knew how to deal with! This sorrow, however, was not coming from any punishment that was handed down directly from the Church. It came from the legal system, the abandonment of my friends, my feelings of regret and concern for the victim, and the heaviness of God's hand upon me.

God certainly used the justice system to punish me far more than any punishment the Church could have inflicted. Sometimes God may use other means and sources to bring about correction or discipline, and it doesn't have to come through the Church (see 1 Pet. 2:13-17). In such a case though, the Church may feel like an ineffective by-stander who didn't put in its two punches.

It need not be that way. The Church, I believe, will always have a role to play, even if it's at the end of the process—rebuke in the presence of all, directing through professional counseling, withholding certain privileges for a period of time, and so forth. This is especially true considering we're God's liaison and instrument of authority here on earth to convince, rebuke, and exhort with all long-suffering and teaching (see 2 Tim. 4:2). We must be careful, however, that we don't pursue punishing people just for the sake of punishment—so we can at least say, "We did punish them." That's not what it's all about.

Though David lived in Old Testament times, his story demonstrates my point. The nation of Israel did not need to stone David and Bathsheba to death for adultery (even though they had biblical grounds to do it) because God had already handed down His decree of punishment that brought devastating pain to David's personal and family life and because David was sincerely repentant (see 2 Sam. 12:9-23; 13; 15; 16–19).

God is most definitely a God of justice, but He's not a legalistic God. God said of the nation of Israel in Jeremiah 30:11,

"For I am with you," says the LORD, "to save you; though I make a full end of all nations where I have scattered you, yet I will not make a complete end of you. But I will correct you in justice, and will not let you go altogether unpunished."

The picture that comes to my mind is like someone standing before a judge facing charges for a crime that has a minimum to maximum sentence range. Within that context, the judge is free to use his discretion. Though he may not give the maximum sentence, he has to at least give the minimum and, therefore, still exercise justice (being just) while at the same time showing a little mercy.

MERCY FOR THE OUTCAST

Jesus had many opportunities where He could have been legalistic. One of those examples is with the woman who had the issue of blood (see Luke 8:43-48). According to the Law of Moses, she was considered unclean (see Lev. 15:19-31) and was to be set apart (pretty much isolated) like a leper. No one was to touch her, everything she lay down on or sat on would be unclean, and anyone who touched her or anything she'd touched would also be unclean. This woman was a woman who, if her situation was public news, would be shunned by others.

After spending all her money on the best physicians without result, she heard that Jesus was passing through town. She had undoubtedly heard about Him and was willing to put her well-being on the line to press through the crowd and touch Him. If someone had known about her situation and had seen her, he could have made things difficult by condemning her—simply opening up her "can of worms" and telling her where to go and where not to go.

She could have cared less! She had already spent all her livelihood without result. If getting results meant she had to endure some onlookers who were critical of her, whether outwardly or inwardly, she was going to press through all of that just to touch Jesus! Who knows, maybe it wasn't that hard to press through the crowds because nobody wanted her to touch them.

The crowd was pushing up against Jesus. When He asked who had touched Him, Peter and the others were incredulous: *"Master, the multitude throng and press You, and You say, 'Who touched Me?'"* (Luke 8:45). Interestingly enough, though many were pressing on Jesus, He only recognized one touch—that of the woman with the issue of blood. Yes, many were touching Him, but only one touched Him with faith. For as she pressed through the crowd from behind, she kept saying to herself, *"If only I may touch His garment, I shall be made well"* (Matt. 9:21).

As soon as she touched Jesus, she was healed, and Jesus could feel the power leaving His body. After Jesus insisted on knowing who had touched Him and she realized that the eyes of the people had zoomed in on her, she fell down before Jesus and trembling, admitted that it was she. Jesus then said to her, *"Daughter, be of good cheer, your faith has made you well. Go in peace"* (Luke 8:48). Jesus could have been legalistic and accused her for not adhering to the Law of Moses. But He didn't. His gracious power ministered to her misery. Thank God for Jesus!

RESTORATION

I'm not an expert or scholar on church discipline and restoration, but I would like to believe I know enough about the Scriptures to understand that God is not a legalist and that He does not promote legalism. The God who loves and promotes justice and who hates partiality is the same God who loves and promotes mercy, truth, grace, and understanding. Didn't God, in His grace, use Jonah to bring about repentance to the people of Nineveh so He could have mercy on them rather than bringing judgment? (See Jonah 3:1-10.)

During my experience, I wasn't looking for the Church to come and pat me on the back while I was carrying my "backpack" of sins. I would not even have been opposed to receiving a public rebuke, which would have been to my own painful benefit and would have helped others to learn and fear. And if the Church had given me the "whip of discipline," hopefully they would have been just as willing to help me heal from the whip. Sadly, what I heard, saw, experienced, and understood personally seemed to indicate that they weren't even willing to administer discipline—they just didn't want anything more to do with me. If anything, there were more ultimatums than evidence of loving, restoring concern through discipline.

The Church of God should certainly exercise justice and discipline based on Scripture, but we shouldn't stop there. We must, in like manner, be just as tenacious (you could even call it "legalistic" in a good sense) when it comes to *restoration* based on Scripture. If all we do is show 100 percent justice and nothing else, God will not be pleased. God's weight of balance is that we be compassionate and merciful too, even in justice. None of us would be so wonderfully saved if God only showed His justice toward us while suppressing His other attributes.

Obedience in the administration of discipline is usually not a problem for the Church. However, following through with the whole package of forgiveness and the reaffirmation of love has seemed to be more difficult and rare. According to Paul, even if we had to turn an immoral brother over to the devil for the destruction of his flesh (see 1 Cor. 5:5), the ultimate goal is still that he would return to the Lord! His soul is still precious to the Lord and is not beyond the delivering power of Almighty God.

Though God hasn't given up on him, if a brother is getting out of hand and refuses to repent, we may have to make some changes in regard to our relationship, association, communication, and so forth. But that doesn't mean we should write him off. Maybe we were at one point just as stiff-necked, but God, being just as stubborn in His love refused to give up on us. The devil may have a degree of liberty in bringing all sorts of destruction in that person's life—possibly even death. But even so, he doesn't have completely free reign to do whatever he wills. The story of Job paints a good picture of this, though from within a somewhat different context (see Job 1–2).

When God brought the sword (enemy, drought, famine, and so forth) against the nation of Israel as a form of punishment, it was always with the desired end that they would come to their senses, realize their situation, rend their hearts, and turn back to Him in repentance. Repentance and restoration are always the desired outcome for God. As the Church, we must seek the same for those who have fallen into sin!

It is a part of the ministry role of the Church to *help* fallen saints deal with the root cause(s) of their sins and to guide them through all the different steps of correction—the ultimate goal always being restoration. There is a difference between a sincerely repentant person and one who knowingly practices and lives in sin, but is unrepentant and shuns reproof. Thus our responses to these two types of people should be rendered accordingly.

We should not turn a blind eye to an immoral brother or sister. There must be correction, discipline, and instruction in righteousness, and it must be done in love and with the intended goal of restoration. What I'm saying is, let us not abandon mercy in order to exercise justice, and let us not abandon justice in order to exercise mercy. We can and should be balanced.

Our Image to the World

The Church is trying to portray holiness to the world by swiftly and sternly dealing with those who are overtaken in sin. Too often this becomes imbalanced, and judgment is enacted with no real concern for the healing of the offending party. But brotherly love and mercy won't fail to take a close look in the mirror. *"For judgment is without mercy to the one who has shown no mercy. Mercy triumphs over judgment"* (James 2:13).

When, for example, top executives, politicians, pro athletes, and famous figures in the world display inappropriate behaviors or practices, most of the time they are immediately dismissed and shunned by their supporters and sponsors. When we do the same, we are responding according to human nature, not God's nature. The Church is called to offer a different way—the opportunity for forgiveness, discipline, healing, and restoration.

HOLINESS DEFINED

Holiness does not mean you don't struggle with sin issues, sometimes even yielding to them. *Holiness* means to be set apart to God, to be sacred or different, to be consecrated. It could also be further defined as when people believe the truth of God's Word and apply it to their lives.

People who have been reconciled to God and have the presence of the Holy Spirit in their lives (leading and guiding them) are holy—even though they may slip from time to time. Holiness is not necessarily behavioral, but rather, relational. *"…If anyone does not have the Spirit of Christ, he is not His"* (Rom. 8:9). Have you been reconciled to God? Are you His child? That is what makes you holy.

Our personal holiness or lack of holiness is a condition of the heart and its expressions. Consider the words of Jesus as He taught the people. He said,

> *You have heard that it was said to those of old, "You shall not commit adultery." But I say to you that whoever looks at a women to lust for her has already committed adultery with her in his heart* (Matthew 5:27-28).

Jesus embodied and fully understood the Scriptures. The purpose of the law was to show us the root problem and the condition of our hearts while directing us to the Lord. But we get caught up focusing on the symptoms, while Jesus goes to the cause and not the manifestation.

Therefore, He says,

"There is nothing that enters a man from outside which can defile him; but the things which come out of him, those are the things that defiles a man..." When He had entered a house away from the crowd, His disciples asked Him concerning the parable. So He said to them, "Are you thus without understanding also? Do you not perceive that whatever enters a man from outside cannot defile him, because it does not enter his heart but his stomach, and is eliminated, thus purifying all foods?" And He said, "What comes out of a man, that defiles a man. For from within, out of the heart of men, proceed evil thoughts, adulteries, fornications, murders, thefts, covetousness, wickedness, deceit, lewdness, and evil eye, blasphemy, pride, foolishness. All these evil things come from within and defile a man" (Mark 7:15-23).

Without God we are nothing; we don't even know what we're capable of. God, in His grace, often delivers us from many traps and evils that would otherwise befall us. For some of us, like me, however, when we become stubborn in our sinful ways, God has a way of letting us have our own way—along with the hurtful consequences.

He doesn't make us do sinful things. We are the ones who choose to entertain sin and its desires. So when God removes His protective restraining grace and we act in sin, we must be humble enough to submit ourselves—not in bitterness, but with a righteous understanding of God's holiness and justice—to His loving, correcting, and restorative discipline. It could also be called "restorative justice." Thus we realize our utter depravity apart from His saving grace in our lives. Only He makes us holy.

A CONTRITE SPIRIT

When I was in the pit of my sinful experience, stories like David's brought great hope to me. I almost believed the lies of the enemy that my sins were too great and that the Lord would not forgive me. But I had to rely on the faithfulness of the Word of God and His promises—that if I confess my sins, He is faithful and just to forgive me of all my sins and cleanse me from all my unrighteousness (see 1 John 1:9).

He said in His Word, *"The Lord is near to those who have a broken heart, and saves such as have a contrite spirit"* (Ps. 34:18)—and that was me. I took much courage from David's story—knowing that if the Lord had forgiven him, He could and would also forgive me.

When I was in jail, I was sharing the love, justice, and grace of God continually. On many occasions the guys would ask me, "How come you're a Christian and you're in here?" At first, I felt lost and embarrassed. I had let the Lord and His people down and weakened my testimony of Him to the point where I felt like I didn't have any right or authority to preach the Gospel. It was challenging.

It was as if the devil was mocking me while God was very displeased with me. But then the Lord gave me strength from His Word and let me know that, though He was hurt, He would not take His mercies from me. My story would not end in jail—my mess would become a message, and my test, a testimony.

My courage was restored, and I began sharing about David, Moses, Peter, Abraham, Judah, Manasseh, Rahab, and so on. It wasn't yet the time or place for me to share my story. To my surprise, most, if not all, of the guys to whom I witnessed (I spoke with quite a few since I was there a few days short of a full year) had only heard the good side of the Bible heroes. They didn't know they were men and women with weaknesses, struggles, and shameful sins.

THE WHOLE MESSY STORY

As I was witnessing to my fellow inmates, I couldn't help but wonder why they didn't know about the other side of some of the greatest heroes in the Bible. Where had the Church dropped the ball? Was it the Sunday school classes, the teaching and preaching from the pulpit, the televangelists, the summer camps, the Vacation Bible School? Or was it the parents who were missing it at home?

God saw how much this disturbed me. As much as I was able to share a more complete story about the saints of old with the inmates, it felt so insignificant and limited. The likelihood was that thousands or millions of people out there have the same one-sided view of the saints. I wanted to do more. And from that desire, the Lord put it on my heart to write this book.

As I talked with these men, I began to feel angry about how one-sided the Gospel presentation has often been. I wasn't angry about my personal experience and how I was treated within the Church community, but I was upset with the greater Church community for being so one-sided about the saints of old, which has greatly affected how we treat each other, especially those who fall, and how we characterize ourselves today.

I'm not on a personal rampage against the Church because I have a "bone" to pick with the saints. Though I have sought to bring some issues into the light, I'm trusting and believing that my criticisms will be constructive and bear fruit in the Church.

My desire and prayer is not to attack the Church, but to help it rise to its fullest potential.

These issues are not limited to me; it's bigger than that. It's about Ted Haggard, Jimmy Swaggart, Jim Bakker, and many others whom you may never hear about because they didn't get the spotlight on CNN. I have been in the Church all my life and have seen a fair share of saints who fell into sin and were treated without the love of Christ—for example, teenage girls and even older women who got pregnant and were scorned and despised. They were treated like they were unregenerate heathen—enemies of the cross.

But Jesus said we're supposed to love even our enemies, to bless those who curse us, to do good to those who hate us, and to pray for those who spitefully use and persecute us (see Matt. 5:44). If we can't even love and restore our own fellow saints who are wounded and hurting because of their sins, but who are members of the Body of Christ, that's troubling!

LOVING THE WHOLE PERSON

Many saints who fall into sin today do so in a much less severe way than David did. Yet many of us cast them off—not wanting anything to do with them. On the other hand, we love to quote David's psalms, sing them in our worship songs, praise God on account of his accomplishments, preach about him, and even desire to be like him and have a greater fellowship with God like he did.

Do we love David only for his achievements, the good side of him, and not as a whole person? People don't come in halves. David was a whole person. If we cannot accept him as the David who sinned with Bathsheba and had her husband killed, then we shouldn't take him as David the psalmist, the man after God's own heart who killed Goliath and became the greatest king in Israel. Am I saying we have to accept David's sins in order to accept him? No. But neither should we cast him off and not accept him just because of his sins. And certainly we should not act as though he never sinned.

I see many who love to play with newborn babies because they're so precious and fun to cuddle up with. They smell so nice and clean. But the moment the baby is poopy, they shun the baby and let him sit in it for hours until the parents come just because they hate the smell of poop and don't like changing diapers. As a parent, I would tell a babysitter like that to straighten up; he or she would certainly not be babysitting my child anymore.

If David was among us today and was to do what he did in ancient Israel, he would not have escaped prison—the remainder of his life and story could very easily have been "life in prison." On the other hand, if God were to permit David to come among us today, we would be very quick to appoint him as pope, general overseer, district overseer, senior pastor, and so forth; he would be nominated and overwhelmingly appointed. On top of that, he would be getting invitations from just about every church to come and minister.

I see a form of hypocrisy among the Body today that is troubling. Saints are crucifying living saints, shooting wounded saints, and glorifying dead saints like David. David really doesn't need the saints' encouragement and support. He's ancient history; his pilgrimage is over. It's those among us who have fallen and need a helping hand who need our support. Why is it that we approve of David the way we now do? Perhaps it is because we know the conclusion of his story.

If a sister among us, who may be a personal friend, falls and puts the Church in the spotlight, and it becomes known that we're friends or members of that Church, what do we do? We don't know what the end of her story will be; does that mean we turn our backs on her? None of us want "friends" who choose not to go through the valley with us, but who, when we get to the mountaintop, want to become very close.

AUTHORITY TO PREACH

Some may say I have no right, place, or authority to address the Church about its shortcomings because, after all, I've committed a horrible and sinful crime. But I would simply ask whether or not Paul had any right, authority, or place to be preaching about Christ and to contend earnestly for the faith—the same faith he had tried to destroy by having some of its messengers put in prison and put to death.

The apostle Peter actually made this plain when he addressed the people who were amazed at the healing of the lame man at Solomon's Porch. He said,

> …*Men of Israel, why do you marvel at this? Or why look so intently at us…? The God of Abraham, Isaac, and Jacob, the God of our fathers, glorified His Servant Jesus, whom you delivered up and* **denied** *in the presence of Pilate, when he was determined to let Him go. But you* **denied** *the Holy One and the Just, and asked for a murderer to be granted to you* (Acts 3:12-14).

It had not been long since Peter had denied Jesus, one of his closest friends. Who was he to be preaching to anybody about denying or not denying Christ? But he could preach about it because he had repented and been forgiven, restored, and justified.

The Scripture says that a minister of the Gospel should have a good testimony in and outside of the Church (see 1 Tim. 3:1-7), and the Bible is the final authority. However, the preaching of the Gospel is not solely based on a person's impeccable record from childbirth, whether in relation to sin or other mistakes. If we had to be perfect to preach, we'd probably preach our own perfectionist, self-righteous version of the Gospel, not that of Christ and salvation through grace by faith.

Paul, who wrote the instructions about leaders to Timothy, did not have an impeccable record. When Jesus first called Paul to be a minister of the Gospel, the Church initially rejected him; they were terrified of him because of his past as a persecutor. But God was able to show the Church His hand of approval on Paul.

The need for a reputable character does not just apply to those who are in leadership, but to all who profess to be Christians (see 1 Pet. 3:15-17). Neither is it a precept that was birthed in the New Testament. David was confronted in his sin by Nathan, the prophet, with these words, "...*by this deed you have given great occasion to the enemies of the LORD to blaspheme...*" (2 Sam. 12:14). God didn't command only the leaders to be holy. He commanded all of the people to be holy (see Exod. 19:10-11; Lev. 11:44-45).

For these reasons, I believe I'm a perfect candidate to address these issues and help the Church find a better way. Not only have I experienced the pain of being rejected by the Church, but I have refused to give up on the Church, and I am doing all I can to work toward restoration in my relationships. I believe things can and should be different, and I believe my testimony and the lessons I've learned can help.

CHAPTER 3

MOSES' STORY

For God's Glory—For My Good

Therefore the LORD will wait, that He may be gracious to you; and therefore He will be exalted, that He may have mercy on you. For the LORD is a God of justice; blessed are all those who wait for Him (Isaiah 30:18).

Before I, Moses, was born, the Lord had destiny, purpose, and greatness predestined for my life. He called me forth from my mother's womb and ordained me to be a prophet, a deliver of His people who were in bondage for over 400 years. It seemed as if the devil was aware of God's plan for my life from the beginning. At my birth, he tried to work through Pharaoh, who ordered the midwives who delivered me and all the Hebrew boy babies to cast us into the Nile River (see Exod. 1:15-21). But God's purpose for my life prevailed against him. The devil knows that there is destiny and greatness in us that will bring glory to God, and he will come after us with fierceness! If he can't kill us, he'll try to mess us up and take us out of God's will. If he can't knock us down and take us out, he'll try to wear us down or out.

God saved me from death by inspiring Pharaoh's daughter to adopt me. I grew up in the palace, but never forgot my people. Deep inside, my anger was stirred up toward the Egyptians because of how they were treating my people. They had no mercy! They made the Hebrews work with rigor in all manner of service—in making bricks and mortar and in laboring in the fields. It was bitter bondage!

IMPATIENT FOR THE PROMISE

I was also angry at God for not hearing the bitter cry of His people and for not delivering us and bringing us into the land that He had promised our forefathers. I had had enough! So when I saw an Egyptian beating one of my countrymen, I glanced quickly to see if anybody was watching me; then I went and killed the Egyptian (see Exod. 2:11-15).

I didn't want to wait for God anymore; we had waited for more than 400 years. So I took things into my own hands and committed murder. My parents knew there was a special calling on my life, and that's why they had put their lives on the line to preserve mine—only to see me grow up and take the life of another.

I remember very well how they told me that after three months of trying to hide me, they had to let me go because they couldn't hide me anymore. I was sent away in the reeds by the bank of the river Nile in a well-prepared ark of bulrushes daubed with asphalt and pitch. Pharaoh's daughter found me and drew me out of the water; hence she gave me the name Moses (which means "to draw forth"). Though my mother was called to take care of me, it was only until I was weaned. After that, I was brought back to Pharaoh's daughter, and she adopted me as her son (see Exod. 2:8-10).

Although I was in the palace of Pharaoh, my mother made sure I knew who I truly was—a child of the promise—a Hebrew. Nevertheless, I was schooled in all the wisdom of the Egyptians, their history, politics, economy, literature, astrology, and so on. I was a prince and judge over the people and became notable in words and deeds.

However, secretly I would study the history of my people and the patriarchs to understand the promise God had made to them. It started to become clearer and clearer that the Lord had chosen me to be the deliverer of His people—especially considering the position I was in. At least that was what I thought.

Many years came and went, and nothing happened. I sought earnestly for every opportunity that would bring me to the place of greater power and authority to deliver the people, but I still ended up destitute. I questioned the God of my fathers: "Who are You? Where are You? Why aren't You taking notice of the people's suffering? I thought You made Your people a promise. I don't see any promise; I see bondage. I don't see any victory; I see defeat and slavery. I don't see any milk and honey (according to Your promise about the Promised Land); I see cucumbers, fish, melons, and onions (the delicacies of Hebrew slaves). If You are who You say You are, fulfill Your promise by delivering Your people and cause them to experience Your goodness." Sadly, they were still in slavery, and it was getting worse!

I couldn't take it anymore—living in the palaces of Egypt while my mother, my other relatives, and my people were breaking their backs under the whip of the Egyptian taskmasters to fortify their country. I was angry at God, but my faith in Him, somehow, came and subdued my anger temporarily.

TAKING IT INTO MY OWN HANDS

One day, in boldness of faith I refused to be called the son of Pharaoh's daughter anymore and went out from the palace, choosing to suffer affliction with my people rather than to remain in the pleasures of sin, which were only for a season. I esteemed the riches of Almighty God and His promises of far greater value than any pleasure Egypt could offer me (see Heb. 11:24-26). It was a trade-off that this world would not understand—giving up what you have as tangible for what you don't have—yet. But faith had it, and I was just waiting on the manifestation.

I humbled myself, giving up the prestigious position as a prince of Egypt, and became a slave along with my people. Their destiny was too great not to be a part of it. Many could not understand why I would do something like that. Some of the Egyptians who knew me called me a fool! Even some of my countrymen joined in with them. I was treated very badly by the taskmasters because they felt that I had betrayed them and that all Egypt had invested in me was in vain. But I knew I had to do what I had to do. I didn't quite understand it all, but I knew it would all work out for God's glory and for my good.

So it happened, when I saw one of the taskmasters beating my countryman, I couldn't hold back my anger anymore, and I killed him. The next day when two of my brethren were fighting each other, I tried to bring peace between them. Then one of them said to me, *"Who made you a prince and judge over us? Do you intend to kill me as you killed the Egyptian?"* (Exod. 2:14). I realized that what I had done must have reached the ears of Pharaoh, so I fled from Egypt to the land of Midian (see Exod. 2:14-15).

THE INTERNAL BATTLE

I was 40 years old when I fled Egypt, and for the next 40 years, I was fighting a raging battle inside of me. Though I had gotten married, had a son, and become a shepherd, my heart was still with my people who were in slavery. I even gave my son the name Gershom so that every time I called his name I would remember that I was a "stranger in a foreign land." For thus was the meaning of his name (see Exod. 2:16-22).

I wanted to be content just being a shepherd and living in Midian, but a part of me refused to be content and settle for less than what the Lord had purposed for my life. He had invested destiny and His glory in me, and what I was going through and the position I found myself in were for my own good—though I didn't know it at the time. When destiny and purpose came calling at the door of my heart, it wouldn't have mattered where I was or how well things might have been going for me, I could not have peace until I found myself on the journey God had for me. God's sustaining and redeeming power truly was greater than my sins.

For 40 years I thought about my people in slavery. I smiled with my family and my in-laws, but deep inside my heart, there was anguish and painful tears! From time to time the memory of killing the Egyptian came back, and with it came thoughts: *You can never be who God has called you to be because you are no longer in Egypt, no longer a prince of Egypt, no longer an influencer of the affairs of Egypt, and no longer admired by the people—not to mention that you broke the law and there is a warrant out for your arrest and possible execution.*

Insurmountable challenges faced me that required the intervention of Almighty God if I would ever fulfill His calling on my life. I was about to learn that God's plan was about His glory, and not mine—but that there was also good in it for me.

The fact was, I took a man's life—and it was not within the context of battle. I didn't steal something that was replaceable; I took a life that I could not restore. The irony to this is that many years later the Lord gave us His laws, which include this one:

He who strikes a man so that he dies shall surely be put to death. However, if he did not lie in wait, but God delivered him into his hand, then I will appoint for you a place where he may flee (Exodus 21:12-13).

The Lord also said,

If he pushes him out of hatred or, while lying in wait, hurls something at him so that he dies, or in enmity he strikes him with his hand so that he dies, the one who struck him shall surely be put to death. He is a murderer... (Numbers 35:20-21).

Were my actions premeditated? You bet they were. Every time I saw an Egyptian beating one of my people, especially the elderly, I had so much indignation in me! I thought of ways to kill and exterminate the Egyptians who were oppressing my people! My fury was not against any specific taskmaster, but all of them in general.

A Divine Encounter

One day, while I was tending the flock of my father-in-law, Jethro, I saw a burning bush. The bush was on fire, but it was not being consumed. So I said to myself, *I must turn aside to see this great sight.* It wasn't until the Lord saw that I had turned that He called to me, "Moses, Moses!" So I replied, "Here I am." Then the Lord began to speak to me about the oppression of His people in Egypt—about their taskmasters and their cry that had come up to Him. He said He had now come down to deliver them, and He was going to send me (see Exod. 3:1-8).

It was a bittersweet ordeal—bitter because He had taken so long and sweet because He had finally come. Nonetheless, I thought to myself, *You have to be joking! There's an arrest warrant in Egypt for me for murder. When I was in the place of power, a prince of Egypt with influence, You didn't call me and use me. But now You want to use me, a shepherd, 40 years later?*

I didn't speak these words to the Lord, but they were welling up inside of me. I didn't want to go back to Egypt. So I thought of excuses for God not to send me, but to send someone else. I told Him I couldn't speak, that I was slow of speech and tongue and not very eloquent—which was not completely true (see Exod. 4:10).

As if the Lord didn't know I wasn't speaking the truth, He declared to me that He was the sovereign God who has created man and who has power over their ability or disabilities (see Exod. 4:11-12). He was not going let me back out. He had this very plan for my life before I was born. He wasn't asking me to go; He was commanding me to go! Whatever excuse I gave, He had an answer. It was the appointed time for the fulfillment of the promise.

I eventually submitted myself to His will, knowing that He had called me for His service and had preserved me for that purpose. I think you know the rest of the story—the ten plagues in Egypt (see Exod. 7–12); the exodus (see Exod. 13–14); the crossing of the Red Sea and the drowning of Pharaoh's army (see Exod. 14); Mount Sinai and the Ten Commandments (see Exod. 19–20); the miraculous provisions in the desert (see Exod. 15–17); the time my anger got the best of me at the rock of Meribah (godly men can lose their cool too—see Num. 20:7-12); and so on.

UNDERSTANDING COMES

For the next 40 years, after my encounter with God at the burning bush, I saw the awesome power of God on behalf of His people. The Lord and I became very close in our relationship. I learnt many things as the Lord taught me and instructed me. He gave me discernment about why He didn't use me when I was in the place of power.

First, there was a specific timeline for how long the Israelites would be in bondage, 400 years (see Gen. 15:12-16), excluding the time of Jacob and his family, because the iniquity of the Amorites was not yet complete, and God was about to use Israel to bring the inescapable judgment on them. Second, God will not share His glory with another (see Isa. 42:8). If He had used me to bring deliverance to Israel during the time when I was a prince of Egypt, the people may have looked to me as their god, and I too probably would have become "big headed." I would have been tempted to take some of the credit, and that would have just set me up for God to bring me down. The Lord waited until I was stripped of everything and humbled—that's when it was the right time for Him and for me. God is not in a rush to accomplish anything. And the best part is that He even redeemed the circumstances of my sin by using them to position me to fulfill my destiny.

RAY'S REFLECTIONS AND INSIGHTS

One aspect of Moses' story, like David's, is the reality that any of us are capable of anything. Moses was a prince, educated and well-respected by the Egyptians. He also loved God and had studied His promises, earnestly desiring to be part of God's plan. He had everything going for him. Yet, in a moment of desperation he became impatient and took things into his own hands, ultimately committing murder. I'm sure he never imagined his story would unfold that way.

In the last chapter, we discussed this at length, but here I want to examine a different side of it. Many people, including saints, are stunned when they see or hear of people of reputable character who give themselves over to unwholesome or criminal activity. Often a neighbor, a relative, or an acquaintance will say, "I never thought he was capable of something like that. I mean, he has always…" or "I've never seen or heard him…" and so forth.

People start to wonder and draw their own conclusions as to what may have led the offender to do such a thing. In a world like Heaven, they probably would have never done something like that. Unfortunately, we live in a sinful world, we have sinful natures that often direct our desires, and the devil and his demons are working nonstop to steal, kill, and destroy (see John 10:10).

WE MUST KNOW OURSELVES

I remember hearing a minister say that if he was Joseph, he more than likely would not have said no to Potiphar's wife when she tried to seduce him (see Gen. 39). I was surprised to hear a minister say that. But I certainly respected him afterward for his blunt honesty. Most saintly brothers would not confess that, but would instead profess their integrity and declare that they would be like Joseph and run. However, though they may be as sincere as can be, the truth is, it's almost impossible to accurately predict our response if and when placed in a situation. I'm not promoting weakness or settling for "whatever will be will be"; I'm just suggesting a humble acknowledgment of our human frailty.

Like Moses, people could be holding back all sorts of feelings, and then suddenly, when it reaches the boiling point, snap at things or people they wouldn't normally snap at. I am sure it wasn't the first time Moses saw a taskmaster beating a Hebrew. But something in him brought him to the point where he couldn't stand seeing it anymore.

Today you may be strong enough to resist certain outbursts of words or deeds because you feel great, spiritually strong, and close to God; you have a good job, and everything is going your way. But then comes a "tomorrow" when all hell is breaking loose. You feel weak and far away from God, you lose your high-paying job, you're about to lose your house, and everything seems to be going the wrong way. With those dynamics in your life, you just don't know how you will respond. You could very easily become peanut butter for someone's bread.

This prayer recorded in Proverbs 30:7-9 admits the truth that many of us may be reluctant to confess.

Two things I request of You (deprive me not before I die): Remove falsehood and lies far from me; give me neither poverty nor riches—feed me with the food allotted to me; lest I be full and deny You, and say, "Who is the LORD?" Or lest I be poor and steal, and profane the name of my God.

Understandably, the application of the context in which I'm sharing these few insights goes far beyond just any one area of sin or temptation for both genders.

Agur, the man who prayed this prayer, understood the deception of the human heart and the reality of its uncertainty when faced with different challenges. He was honest about what the possibility of being rich or poor might cause him to do or not do.

Some of us would be quick to declare with utmost certainty that we would never steal anything, no matter what! But we shouldn't be so quick to say that. Unless we have been to the point of severe hunger and starvation, almost to the point of death, and had opportunity to steal food for our survival, but did not, we are simply declaring something in ignorance. The truth is, we just don't know what our actions would be. On one occasion, things got so bad for the nation of Israel that two women made a pact to eat their sons to avoid starvation—and did end up eating one of them (see 2 Kings 6:25-31). According to Proverbs 28:21, a man will transgress even for a piece of bread.

It's good to have confidence in our integrity and have predetermined convictions as to what we will or will not do. I'm all for that. But only God knows our limits. Some of those same saintly brothers who are so confident that they would run from Potiphar's wife would only make one step and then fall right back into her waiting arms.

Most likely Potiphar had one of the most beautiful women in the land of Egypt. Such high ranking officials don't just marry any woman off the street. They normally had the privilege of choosing whoever they wanted as a wife from a select group of beautiful women. Certainly they would have chosen the most outwardly beautiful ones. To consistently resist someone of that nature (like

Joseph did) would not have been the easiest thing to do—but for the grace of God. I am not saying that men or women in general don't have integrity, just that temptation is real and we are all susceptible. I do believe there are 21st-century Josephs and Ruths. I even believe you can find them outside the Church.

A Lesson From Esau

Nevertheless, in case it seems like I'm a little out on the deep end, let me share an example from the Bible that differs a bit in nature, but has far-reaching principles that go beyond just food.

Esau was a skilled hunter, a man of the fields, while his brother, Jacob, was a mild man, dwelling in tents—a home boy, in other words. One day Esau went out hunting and came back feeling weary and hungry (maybe because he hadn't made a kill that day and had exerted all his energy). Esau came home and saw his brother making a delicious pot of stew. Being weary and hungry, Esau politely asked his brother for some of his stew.

Jacob responded by asking Esau to sell him his birthright in exchange for some of the stew. (Esau was the oldest brother and was, therefore, the rightful heir of the blessing and inheritance according to the tradition of those days.)

Esau then said to Jacob, *"Look, I am about to die; so what is this birthright to me?"* (Gen. 25:32). In a moment of weariness and hunger (he wasn't even at the point of starvation, just hungry), Esau despised and gave up the birthright that should have been precious to him—just for a plate of food. Jacob made Esau swear to him as he sold him his birthright, and then Jacob gave him bread and lentil stew. Thus Esau ate and drank, then arose and left.

On a normal day of victory, when Esau had made a kill and was not feeling weary and hungry, but was feeling great because of his success, it's unthinkable that Esau would have sold his birthright. Instead, he would have been able to see through his brother's conniving bait instead of focusing on the temporary satisfaction of his gut! The same could be said of many of us in our own varying contexts. I know I can say it about myself.

DIVINE PROTECTION

The point is, far too often we take the glory for walking in integrity, holiness, and so forth. But First Corinthians 10:13 clearly states that

No temptation has overtaken you except such as is common to man; but God is faithful, who will not allow you to be tempted beyond what you are able, but with the temptation will also make the way of escape, that you may be able to bear it.

It can't get any plainer than that; it is *God* who causes us not to be tempted beyond what we are able to bear. This indicates that we all have a breaking point where we will yield to sin. It is God who provides the escape routes and gives the strength so we can both bear up under it and escape it. So it is not really our integrity that deserves the glory, but God Almighty—the Shepherd of our souls. When we wrongly give ourselves credit for our holiness, we make ourselves vulnerable, perhaps even removing ourselves from God's protecting, escape-route-providing hand.

Many, including me, have presumptuously planned to sin—against our own conscience and the commands of the Lord—but God intervened. A phone call changed everything. Or maybe it was a dream, a sermon that the pastor preached, a flat tire, an accident, a Scripture you read in your morning devotions, a snow storm, a debit card displaying "insufficient funds," the loss or acquiring of a new job—you name it. God can use countless scenarios to cancel a potential manifestation of sin.

Some could see these events as just a matter of coincidence, which they may be at times. Others will accept them as divine intervention—God trying to deliver us from sinning against Him and thereby saving us and possibly others from pain and hurt.

PURSUIT OF SIN

David also made note of the deceitfulness of the human heart and its boldness to pursue willful sin:

Who can understand his errors? Cleanse me from secret faults. Keep back Your servant also from presumptuous sins; let them not have dominion over me. Then I shall be blameless, and I shall be innocent of great transgression. Let the words of my mouth and the meditation of my heart be acceptable in Your sight, O LORD, my strength and my Redeemer (Psalm 19:12-14).

My understanding is that it's not only criminals who commit crimes, but also people of credible reputation and integrity. No one is born a criminal; they become criminal. As we talked about in the chapter on David, anybody is capable of anything. All it takes is for people's circumstances to change. Suddenly they find themselves surrounded by mountains, the Red Sea, and a mighty army like Pharaoh's (figuratively speaking). I believe there can be multiple reasons that cause a person to go from one side of the spectrum to the next in a matter of seconds, minutes, days, or even years. I wonder how long it took Moses to go from a respectable, high-ranking prince of Egypt to a murderer.

Right after my sinful actions that landed me in jail, I heard that the Bible college I had attended was thinking about the possibility of screening future students before accepting them. It may sound great, but I doubt it would work. This kind of screening is always based on the habits, behaviors, or traits of a person's past, with the goal of giving us a reasonable assumption as to what that person may or may not be capable of. However, screening will not pick up anything questionable from the "perfect" student (like the well-trained and educated prince of Egypt—Moses).

Some are already known as criminals, while some will become criminals. It's not always so easy to predict who will or will not become one. Often we are proven wrong in our selection and assumption. The person whom we think may be a good role model turns out to be a bad one, and the one we thought would be a bad one, turns out to be a good one. It happens. No one would've called Moses a criminal or predicted his slaying of the Egyptian. But he did it nonetheless.

According to our judicial system, we are all innocent until proven guilty. According to the Bible, we are all capable of being guilty, no matter how good we look on the outside. Thus, any projecting of the likelihood of sinful or criminal activity in a person's life overlooks the fact that we are all likely sinners and criminals apart from God's grace and saving hand.

FACING FAILURE WITH GOD

When Christians fall into sin, facing our shortcomings is one of the hardest, most terrible pains. I'm sure Moses struggled with this during his 40 years in the desert. He must have felt like a complete failure with no hope of a meaningful future. Like him, we are repentant, but feel as though our lives can never be redeemed.

We have forfeited our destiny; the damage is irreparable. But God will face our mistakes, sinful or not, with us, if we will let Him. He certainly did it with Moses; and He's doing it with me.

When I was in jail, I felt that after I was released I should just be content to be a failure with a criminal record. I had blown it. I was in the place of influence and was admired by many, though certainly not as Moses was. I had, through my own making, made what was once possible, impossible. But even when I wanted to turn a deaf ear to the majestic voice of the Lord, His voice was too penetrating. I was in the palm of His hand. Though at times I felt like letting go, He would not let me go. Being delayed did not mean I was denied. Very few stories in the Bible exemplify this truth as does Moses' story. I was encouraged that God is the God of second chances. I'm so thankful He didn't let me go even when I wanted to!

I'm truly grateful that our relationship with the Lord is not subject to us turning away from Him whenever we feel like it. It is not like the relationship that we often see between couples and friends, when one says, "I've had enough; I can't take this anymore—I'm out of here!" Then the other one might say something like, "Fine! If you want to go, go! It won't be the end of the world! There are other fish in the sea."

Thanks be to God that our Lord is not like that. His relentless love and promise pursues us as seen in the story of Moses and in the Book of Hosea. The Lord commanded Hosea to go and love a woman—a woman at the bottom of the list of potential wives—a prostitute named Gomer. But Hosea did, and they had children together. Unfortunately, Gomer left Hosea and went back to her lifestyle of harlotry. But the Lord told Hosea to pursue her and buy her back.

...Go again, love a woman who is loved by a lover and is committing adultery, just like the love of the LORD for the children of Israel...So I bought her for myself for fifteen shekels of silver, and one and one-half homers of barley. And I said to her, "You shall stay with me many days; you shall not play the harlot, nor shall you have a man—so, too, will I be toward you" (Hosea 3:1-3).

This is the same unconditional, pursuing love that caused Jesus to come with the purpose of seeking and saving those who are lost—sinners. He is the kindest, most gracious person we will ever know. And He never gives up on us, just as Hosea never gave up on Gomer. He didn't give up on Moses or David, and He won't give up on us.

THE LORD PARDONS

The world would not pronounce the apostle Paul innocent of the blood of Stephen, who was stoned to death, and the many others who were martyred under his persecution of the Church (see Acts 7:54-8:1-3). Even the Church rejected Paul at the beginning; they were suspicious of him, wondering whether his conversion was genuine, because of his history as a persecutor (see Act. 9:1-30). But in the eyes of the Lord, he was redeemed and justified, and the Church was on its way to recognizing that.

Many Christians may not understand the redeeming, restoring, and justifying love and power of God. When God redeems, pardons, and justifies, it's as if we never sinned. The blood of Jesus literally pays for (cancels) our sins so that they are wiped from the record.

Paul understood his position in Christ; therefore, he was able to stand against any accusation. We also must know our place in

Christ to be able to stand against the condemnation of the world and the devil. *"As far as the east is from the west, so far has He removed our transgressions from us"* (Ps. 103:12).

Though Paul confessed that his zeal in persecuting the Church was done ignorantly in unbelief (see 1 Tim. 1:12-14), he also said,

> *This is a faithful saying and worthy of all acceptance, that Christ Jesus came into the world to save sinners, of whom I am chief. However, for this reason I obtained mercy, that in me first Jesus Christ might show all longsuffering, as a pattern to those who are going to believe on Him for everlasting life* (1 Timothy 1:15-16).

Moses, too, could have questioned his ability to lead Israel after his fall into sin. Perhaps this is the real reason behind his excuses at the burning bush for why God should send someone else (see Exod. 4:10-12). But Moses knew better. He learned first-hand the incredible mercy of God. He knew that even though he had failed he could still lead and encourage others to be faithful. When believers don't deal with the sin in their lives by making it right with God and turning away from their wicked ways—they become hypocrites because their "past" is still in their present. But those who have turned away from their sin, regardless of how repetitive or shameful it was, are not hypocrites. The blood of Jesus redeems them.

GOD'S GLORY, OUR GOOD

Moses shows us how God really can work all things together for our good. Though Moses sinned by killing the Egyptian, God used the time Moses spent hiding in the desert to prepare him for his calling. Being a shepherd prepared him for what God had in store for him—shepherding the children of Israel. He thought he was in the desert and not accomplishing anything, but God was preparing him for His purpose.

That is often how He prepares His children for their destiny. I pray I will be able to testify that God also completely redeemed my time in prison by using it to prepare me for my life call.

The apostle Paul wrote,

For you see your calling, brethren, that not many wise according to the flesh, not many mighty, not many noble, are called. But God has chosen the foolish things of the world to put to shame the wise, and God has chosen the weak things of the world to put to shame the things which are mighty; and the base things of the world and the things which are despised God has chosen, and the things which are not, to bring to nothing the things that are, that no flesh should glory in His presence...that, as it is written, "He who glories, Let him glory in the LORD" (1 Corinthians 1:26-31).

These words are also echoed in the story of Gideon:

And the LORD said to Gideon, "The people who are with you are too many for Me to give the Midianites into their hands, lest Israel claim glory for itself against Me, saying 'My own hand has saved me'" (Judges 7:2).

Gideon had 32,000 soldiers, and God said the army was too big and would take the glory if victorious. So the Lord brought the army down to 300 men, and with the 300 men, God caused Gideon to defeat an army of over 135,000 men—that's God! He will always resist the proud, but He will always give His grace to the humble (see 1 Pet. 5:5).

The Lord purposefully hardened Pharaoh's heart so that He could make Himself known among the Egyptians, His people Israel, all peoples of the earth, and all generations to come. God is not uncertain about who He is; He knows Himself. That's why He said, "My name is I Am who I Am." The Israelites didn't really know Him; they didn't know that He was and is everything they could ever need and more. God is forever the same; He will not and cannot increase or decrease in any aspect of who He is. Rather than God taking forever just to tell us who He is, the provider, the healer, our peace, defense, righteousness, creator, savior, joy, and so forth, He just said, "I Am Who I Am"—God (see Exod. 3:13-14).

How will we know that God is a God of the impossible if we're always faced with what is possible? If we're always faced with the possible, then we won't really need God; we could just do it ourselves. He will not share His glory with us, and that's often why He allows us to come up against impossible mountains. There He can show Himself strong on our behalf and be glorified, and there we will remain humble and trusting in Him—it is for our own good.

When Israel was fighting the Amalekites, if Moses raised his hands, Israel was winning, but when his arms got tired and began falling, the enemy started winning. Moses needed help to keep his arms raised so Aaron and Hur brought a rock for him to sit on, and then they each went under his arms and helped to support him until the sun went down and Israel got the victory. This, I'm sure, was also to keep Moses humble and to remind him not to think too much of himself (see Exod. 17:8-13).

God even chose to bury and hide Moses' body for His own glory. Satan would have liked to get a hold of his body and cause the nation of Israel to possibly mummify it or make a shrine to it—worshiping it like they did the golden calf and the snake on the pole that was used to heal them in the wilderness (see Exod. 32:1-6; Num. 21:4-9; 2 Kings 18:1-4). By worshiping the calf and the snake, Israel gave God's glory to satan, which was not to their benefit. God certainly demonstrated through Moses' life that He is jealous for His glory, but that when He has taught us humility, He will use us in ways we can hardly imagine, to do things we could never dream of!

All the humbling experiences that Moses went through were perhaps the reason why the Scripture asserts this fact about him after Miriam and Aaron rose up against him, *"Now the man Moses was very humble, more than all men who were on the face of the earth"* (Num. 12:3).

BLESSED TO BE A BLESSING

We must realize that God is a redeemer, not only of people, but also of situations. Even the gravest sins He can turn around and use for His purposes. This does not mean that the sinful actions were His plan, but only that He can redeem our mistakes. True ministers will understand this and will help those who have fallen to get back on their feet so they can see God redeem their lives and circumstances.

Fallen saints, when restored, will actually be an asset to the Church; they may be better able to sympathize with and help others who fall. Though Christ did not fall by sinning, He was tempted in all points as we are. In His omniscience, He understands the state of the saints who are tempted and who may fall into sin, as well as the sinners who need salvation.

Christ was aware of the importance of being able to relate to us. The Word of God says,

> *Therefore, in all things He had to be made like His brethren, that He might be a merciful and faithful High Priest in things pertaining to God, to make propitiation for the sins of the people. For in that He Himself has suffered, being tempted, He is able to aid those who are tempted* (Hebrews 2:17-18).

> *For we do not have a High Priest who cannot sympathize with our weaknesses, but was in all points tempted as we are, yet without sin. Let us therefore come boldly to the throne of grace, that we may obtain mercy and find grace to help in time of need* (Hebrews 4:15-16).

Paul also said,

> *Blessed be the God and Father of our Lord Jesus Christ, the Father of mercies and God of all comfort, who comforts us in all our tribulation, that we may be able to comfort those who are in any trouble, with the comfort with which we ourselves are comforted by God* (2 Corinthians 1:3-4).

We are blessed to be a blessing, and God often comforts us so that we will be of comfort to someone else.

Spreading the Message

This idea of redemption is central to the Gospel, yet too often we have minimized the sins in the lives of the characters in Bible stories, thus watering down (in our interpretation) the saving power of God. Seeing Moses not only as a victorious deliverer and leader who God talked with face-to-face, but also as a redeemed murderer, gives us a much fuller picture of the grace of God in Moses' life. And it gives us hope for ourselves.

Many animated movies are being made about Bible heroes. These often have a wonderful message, geared mainly toward children, but children will grow up. The shortcoming in these shows or movies, for the most part, is that they portray Bible heroes as perfect people. They don't tell the whole story—they don't communicate that there was another side to these characters, that they were real people with real struggles. Certainly, this should be done in an age-appropriate manner, but the fact that sin is ugly does not mean we should never teach our children about it.

In the story of Moses, the killing of the Egyptian usually is highlighted because it was a pivotal part of his life that separated Moses the sinner in Egypt from Moses the saint whom God apprehended in the wilderness. However, the other side of many other Bible heroes isn't as clearly revealed. I'm not saying we should go around exposing every sin we can find about the Bible heroes, but if we omit the facts, we can inadvertently teach people that saints are saints because they are sinless and perfect. The balanced, realistic portrayal shows that they sinned too.

In the family of God, revealing the other side of each other should never be done to bring shame; rather, it is to give hope to others and to show the grace and justice of our Lord. People don't just tell stories for the sake of telling stories—there's a reason behind it. Stories told in their context, never mind the subject (though I say this with love and understanding), must be purposeful in their objective to expose the justice of God, the mercy of God, the grace of God, and the unconditional love of God.

Bible heroes sinned. They fell, they made mistakes, they struggled, they felt lonely at times, they felt like giving up at times, they had fears and insecurities, and so forth. Some of them were even suicidal at different points. Job and Jeremiah, at certain points in their lives, wished they weren't even born (see Job 3:1-13; Jer. 20:14-18). We must also realize that the Bible does not give a comprehensive record of anyone's life. The fact that the Bible doesn't record any flaws or sins in the life of Daniel, for example, does not imply that he was sinless and perfect. None of the heroes of the faith were, though some definitely stand out as being more sinful and some as more faithful.

Many Christians look to Bible heroes as role models, and they beat up on themselves because they feel so far away from attaining the status that these Bible heroes attained. If they only knew the other side of these men and women of God, it might bring great consolation and encouragement. With that being said, I would encourage everyone reading this book, whether you're a Christian or not, to look into the Bible for yourself. Try reading the Bible from front to back. By so doing, you will know the whole truth— that darker, less familiar side of the journeys of Bible heroes.

For those of us who are Christians, it is our duty to read, study, and meditate upon the Word of God (see Ps. 1:1-3; 1 Tim. 4:12-16; 2 Tim. 2:15; 3:14-15). Too many of us just take whatever the preacher says without matching it up to the Scriptures. According to Acts 17:10-12, the believers didn't just receive the word with readiness; they also searched the Scriptures daily to find out whether those things were so. What the preacher preaches should be reaffirmation, confirmation, and possibly further insight, not necessarily new revelation.

Even if God calls a fool, He's going to put that fool through God's "school." In other words, God will call anybody, but He has no intention of leaving them in their original state. He will change, break, mold, equip, anoint, inspire, and empower for the glory of His name.

CHAPTER 4

MANASSEH'S STORY

God's Grace Is Greater

 The LORD is merciful and gracious, slow to anger, and abounding in mercy. He will not always strive with us, nor will He keep His anger forever. He has not dealt with us according to our sins, nor punished us according to our iniquities (Psalm 103:8-10).

Evil and wickedness were enthroned during my reign as king of Judah and Jerusalem. I, Manasseh, was guilty of breaking just about every commandment and law of God. I surpassed the evil and wickedness of the Canaanites who dwelt in the Promised Land before the children of Israel. Not surprisingly, I was given the title as "one of Judah's most wicked kings"! Gratefully, though, I found out that God's grace was still greater than all my sins!

My father, Hezekiah, was a great man of God. He loved and feared the Lord and accomplished great things for Him—though he himself had his own mishaps. It was prophetically declared to him to get his house in order because his death was imminent; he was suffering from a severe disease. Upon hearing this prophecy, he humbled himself and cried out to the Lord for mercy. So the Lord heard him and had compassion on him, granting him 15 more years (see 2 Kings 20:1-11).

NOT IN MY FATHER'S FOOTSTEPS

Interestingly enough, it was during these 15 years of grace that I was born. Unfortunately, I was the complete opposite of my father. Maybe if my father had been alive to see all the evil and wickedness that engulfed my life, he would have regretted not surrendering himself to the word of the Lord and going to his rest when the Lord was ready to take him home. I'm sure my father would admit that the Lord may have seen my birth on the horizon, as well as one of my father's greatest sins—allowing the Babylonians to view the articles and treasures of his house (see 2 Kings 20:12-18). Perhaps the Lord was trying to spare him and the nation the misery—because I certainly brought misery on the land!

I did not follow in his godly footsteps. I made a complete 180 degree turn from the things of my father. Where he had established righteousness, I replaced it with wickedness and unrighteousness. Where he had instituted the fear of God, I instituted worship of many other gods. It was awful!

I am one of the greatest examples that "like father, like son" isn't always true. You can be a God-fearing, righteous man who is diligent in teaching the things of the Lord to your son, but that doesn't mean he will automatically follow in your legacy. He still has free will and may choose to rebel. The first example of this is evident between God and Adam in the Garden of Eden.

If you do your part as a father or mother, God will not hold you accountable for any evil that your children may plunge themselves into, especially when they're grown and on their own. Nonetheless, in spite of what they may or may not do, you must never write them off from the grace of God. His grace will always be greater—period.

I was 12 years old when I became king of Judah, and I reigned 55 years in Jerusalem in my father's place. From the very outset of my kingship, I introduced wickedness. The Bible summarizes the evil story of my life this way: *"...But he did evil in the sight of the LORD, according to the abominations of the nations whom the LORD had cast out before the children of Israel"* (2 Chron. 33:2).

God was not bored and wanting to see some killing sprees for entertainment when He commanded the Israelites to kill all the inhabitants of the land they were going to possess. The severity, extent, and duration of their evil and wicked abominations were unbearable before God, and He used the Israelites to bring judgment against them (see Lev. 18:24-27). God often uses one nation to punish another nation, not to mention famine and other forms of natural disasters.

Their sexuality was perverse, and their religious practices, which often correlated with their sexuality, were also perverse! Occult practices and rituals, including child sacrifice, bestiality, incest, and all different forms of astrology, witchcraft, and demonic worship were rampant.

So what exactly did I do? Well, I reinstated all the idolatrous worship that my father had abolished, along with rebuilding their altars, which were mainly called "high places." Besides these things, I raised up altars for Baal (a chief god of the Canaanites and supposedly the god of nature) and made brand-new wooden images. All of these acts were in blatant disobedience to the first and second commandments.

> *You shall have no other gods before Me. You shall not make for yourself a carved image—any likeness of anything that is in heaven above, or that is in the earth beneath, or that is in the water under the earth; you shall not bow down to them nor serve them. For I, the LORD your God, am a jealous God...* (Exodus 20:3-5).

I was a devout worshiper of idols. I worshiped, served, and built altars for all the host of Heaven, which the Lord had strictly commanded us not to do, saying in Deuteronomy 4:19,

> *And take heed, lest you lift up your eyes to heaven, and when you see the sun, the moon, and the stars, all the host of heaven, you feel driven to worship them and serve them, which the LORD your God has given to all the peoples under the whole heaven as a heritage.*

Without any fear of Almighty God, my evil heart became more evil and dared me to build altars of worship within the temple of the Lord and also in the temple courtyards. In the Israeli sacrificial system, if a priest failed to dress, eat, wash his hands, groom his hair and beard properly, abstain from drinking strong drinks, or perform the sacrifice and follow-up procedures correctly, it could be the difference between living or dying for him.

Within this sacrificial system, the priests had to sacrifice an animal whenever they were guilty of sinning, and on the Day of Atonement, the high priest had to first offer a sin offering for himself and his household, and then for the entire nation. This put to rest any speculation or false pretense on the part of the priests that they were sinless and perfect saints of God. God knew that not even the leaders and ministers were so perfectly sanctified that they couldn't sin—even if it was unintentional (see Lev. 4; 16).

CHILD SACRIFICE AND WITCHCRAFT

One of the most heartless and coldblooded things I did was sacrifice my sons in the fire to my gods! I called it a sincere ritual sacrifice of religious obedience, but God called it murder! The Lord had instructed Moses in Leviticus 20:2 saying,

> *Again, you shall say to the children of Israel, "Whoever of the children of Israel, or of the strangers who dwell in Israel, who gives any of his descendants to Molech* [the god who received child sacrifices], *he shall surely be put to death. The people of the land shall stone him with stones."*

The Lord had also said,

> *You shall not worship the LORD your God in that way; for every abomination to the LORD which He hates they have done to their gods; for they even burn their sons and daughters in the fire to their gods* (Deuteronomy 12:31).

As if my sons were animals, I sacrificed them to the gods. According to the Word of God, because of this practice, I was deserving of death. Not only did I sacrifice my sons, but much innocent blood was shed upon the land at my command. I also led many of the people of Judah into sin. I had no sense of account-ability to anyone except the gods. I did whatever I wanted. By so doing, I made Ahab and the other wicked kings of Israel and Judah look like they were students of evil and I was the teacher.

My evil, rebellious heart did not stop at human sacrifice; it took me even further. Although the Word of God clearly forbids any form of occult practice, I got deeply engrossed in it. The law declared,

> *There shall not be found among you anyone who makes his son or his daughter pass through the fire, or one who practices witchcraft, or a soothsayer, or one who interprets omens, or a sorcerer, or one who conjures spells, or a medium, or a spiritist, or one who calls up the dead. For all who do these things are an abomination to the LORD, and because of these abominations the LORD your God drives them out from before you* (Deuteronomy 18:10-12).

The occult should not be taken lightly. But I did take it lightly, and I foolishly got involved with it, thinking that it wouldn't harm me and that God was not aware of it. The occult, manifesting in many different forms, is one of the enemy's main forces of influence in the earth, and it has been present in every generation. Some of the people who followed my example may have thought it was just a game, but I knew it was as real as the air we breathe. If it wasn't real, God would not have warned us against these practices and the power and reality of them.

As the evil and wicked details of my life came close to their end, the Lord said concerning me, "*...he has acted more wickedly than all the Amorites who were before him, and has also made Judah sin with his idols...*" (2 Kings 21:11). My life was an abominable reproach to the Lord! To make things even worse, beside my personal sins, I had caused Judah and the people of Jerusalem to do more evil than the nations who were before us, whom the Lord had destroyed!

That was my evil reputation, and it pretty much sums up my wicked life. You can't become much more sinful and evil than I was. The sins of my life were not just vast in number, but also in severity.

Graciously and fortunately, I did not go to my grave in that state. The Lord doesn't bring immediate judgment without giving a person or nation warning and time to repent. Many times prophets would come and declare warning, repentance, calamity, and judgment to me, but it never fazed me. I had dreams and different things happening around me that, if I had been interested and willing, I could have clearly seen that the Lord was trying to get my attention. God does not delight in showing wrath or judgment, but He does delight in showing mercy. Micah puts it this way,

> *Who is a God like You, pardoning iniquity and passing over the transgression of the remnant of His heritage? He does not retain His anger forever, because He delights in mercy. He will again have compassion on us, and will subdue our iniquities. You will cast all our sins into the depths of the sea* (Micah 7:18-19).

The Lord delights more in forgiving sins than He does in judging them—though the sins must be dealt with. Good parents do not enjoy or look forward to disciplining their children. Rather, those parents would prefer, when their children make a mistake, that they would come to them and confess and ask for forgiveness. But sometimes it takes disciplinary action from the parents to allow the children to see the seriousness of their mistakes—only then are they willing to take responsibility, confess, repent, and change.

After many failed attempts to get my attention, the Lord sent calamity and judgment on me personally, but also on all the land of Judah. The Lord brought the captains of the army of the king of Assyria against the people of Judah and Jerusalem with much destruction. I was taken captive to Babylon, bound with hooks and bronze fetters. Marching on the long journey toward the land of my captivity, in the heat of the sun and the coolness of nightfall, I had lots to think about and a lot of time to do it.

I was humiliated, disgraced, and dethroned from my kingdom. I was literally brought to my knees! It was unlike anything I'd ever experienced or anticipated. Cold, lonely, hungry, and filthy, I was in affliction! The burdensome affliction began weighing heavily on my heart, and all of its evil substance was being squeezed to the surface for me to deal with face-to-face. All I had done was surrounding me like a mirror of guilt, reproach, rejection, and condemnation. I was confronted with who I really was and had become. My past caught up to my present and started to condemn me. It was a horrible feeling and experience!

In the midst of my dilemma of judgment, I remembered the God of my fathers. I remembered that the God of Abraham, Isaac, and Jacob is a gracious and awesome God who pardons iniquity and transgressions. His anger is not forever because He delights in mercy. I also remembered the period of the judges and their cycle of repentance and restoration, of sin and rebellion followed by affliction and judgment—and I remembered that every time they turned to the Lord He answered them.

Furthermore, I recalled the prayer of my ancestral father, Solomon, and how the Lord accepted his prayer:

When they sin against You (for there is no one who does not sin), and You become angry with them and deliver them to the enemy, and they take them captive to a land far or near; yet when they come to themselves in the land of where they were carried captive, and repent, and make supplication to You in the land of their captivity, saying, "We have sinned, we have done wrong, and have committed wickedness"; and when they return to You with all their heart and with all their soul... and pray toward their land which You gave to their fathers... and toward the temple which I have built for Your name: then hear from heaven Your dwelling place their prayer and their supplications, and maintain their cause, and forgive your people who have sinned against You (2 Chronicles 6:36-39).

My pride was humbled, and my strength was weakened. The king, the big macho man that I thought I was, became fragile and fell to pieces. I wept bitterly! Literally on my knees and face, I poured out my heart and soul in tears to the Lord! I acknowledged and confessed all my abominable sins and wickedness—my rebellion, idolatry, occult practices, murder, stubbornness, and the way I led the people to sin.

I knew the Lord would hear my prayer because it was on the basis of His Word, and my confession of tears, in remorse and repentance, was from a broken and sincere heart. I was convinced I hadn't done anything, whether in number or severity, that could surpass the grace of God. His grace was simply far greater than any and all of my sins!

If any person ever had reason to be hopeless, it would have been me. Nevertheless, I refused to die in my hopelessness! My sins and wickedness could not surpass, drown out, or outdo the loving grace of God! He said in His Word, *"I, even I, am He who blots out your transgressions for My own sake; and I will not remember your sins"* (Isa. 43:25).

I knew His love for me was unconditional and His grace was not limited. Though I knew He loved me, I knew He was also greatly displeased and grieved over the things I had done.

During this time, I also recalled this prayer:

Will You work wonders for the dead? Shall the dead arise and praise You? Shall Your loving-kindness be declared in the grave? Or Your faithfulness in the place of destruction? Shall Your wonders be known in the dark? And Your righteousness in the land of forgetfulness? (Psalm 88:10-12)

So I began to ask the Lord to show me the mercy and grace that He said He delights in and had so often demonstrated to my forefathers. What happened after I sought the Lord in my afflictions is recorded in Second Chronicles 33:12-16:

Now when he was in affliction, he implored the LORD his God, and humbled himself greatly before the God of his fathers, and prayed to Him; and He received his entreaty, heard his supplication, and brought him back to Jerusalem into his kingdom. Then Manasseh knew that the Lord was God. After this he built a wall outside the City of David on the west side of Gihon, in the valley, as far as the entrance of the Fish Gate.... He took away the foreign gods and the idol from the house of the LORD, and all the altars that he had built in the mount of the house of the LORD and in Jerusalem; and he cast them out of the city. He also repaired the altar of the LORD, sacrificed peace offerings and thank offerings on it, and commanded Judah to serve the LORD God of Israel.

I made a lot of vows to the Lord saying what I would and wouldn't do if He delivered me from bondage. I said, like the Psalmist, *"I will go into Your house with burnt offerings; I will pay*

You my vows, which my lips have uttered and my mouth has spoken when I was in trouble" (Ps. 66:13-14). But of course God's grace did not attend to me based on the degree of my vows, but based on who He is. As it says in Psalm 147:10-11, *"He does not delight in the strength of the horse; He takes no pleasure in the legs of a man. The LORD takes pleasure in those who fear Him, in those who hope in His mercy."* Though I lived most of my life wrongly, by the end I had learned the fear of the Lord and the hope of His mercy!

Ray's Reflections and Insights

Manasseh's story holds many lessons for us. One of the most sobering lessons springs from the fact that Manasseh was able to build altars and worship idols right inside the temple of God without the Lord striking him down. That should not have been possible. I believe Manasseh got away with it because God's glory was not there. The glory of His manifest presence makes the difference.

Many of us are crying out to God, individually and collectively, for more of His glory in our lives. But are we willing and ready to commit ourselves to sustaining the weight of that glory? When the Shechinah glory (the manifest presence of God) showed up at the initial dedication of the temple, the worship team and worshipers, along with the priests, could not stand under the weight of His awesome power and glory. Instead they fell on their knees with their faces to the ground in worship (see 2 Chron. 5:2-14; 2 Sam. 6:1-11).

We must make a conscious choice to deal with our own sins and judge ourselves according to First Corinthians 11:31, Hebrews 12:1-6, and First John 1:9-10. Then we'll be ready and positioned for the weight of God's glory. If the Lord began pouring out a much greater degree of His glory in the Church today, would much of what is currently going on be able to continue?

Would the churches that are ordaining homosexual bishops and performing same-sex marriages be able to continue in like manner? I think not. God does not hate the homosexuals, but He hates their homosexual practice the same way He hated Manasseh's idolatry, witchcraft, and so forth. God is able to look beyond (not overlook or condone) the sins of the saints and still love us. He is just as able to look beyond the sins of the sinners and love them. If God was not able or willing to do that, none of us would be saved.

None of us are saved in our sins, but apart from our sins. God is not out to save the sinful nature, but to kill it and replace it with His nature. Therefore, practicing religion in and of itself is not God's will for humankind. His will is that each of us would know Him personally by being reconciled to Him through forgiveness of sins and by expressing our love and gratefulness to Him through repentance and obedience.

This is what Jesus said to the people,

Not every one who says to Me, "Lord, Lord," shall enter the kingdom of heaven, but he who does the will of My Father in heaven. Many will say to Me in that day, "Lord, Lord, have we not prophesied in Your name, cast out demons in You name, and done many wonders in Your name?" And then I will declare to them, "I never knew you; depart from Me, you who practice lawlessness!" (Matthew 7:21-23)

INTO CAPTIVITY

One of the most compelling parts of Manasseh's story, for me, is his experience of going into captivity because it reminds me of my own captivity in prison. When I first got to the prison, I was placed in a cell with a bunk bed and another inmate. Approximately half the cells on that unit, about 17 or 18, were single cells, and the others were double—with bunk beds. Whenever a single cell became available, someone from the double cell would move into it on a "seniority" first-come, first-served basis. This was the case both on the remand unit where I stayed during trial procedures and in the population units where I went after I was convicted and sentenced.

The first cell they put me in was a double cell, cell number three. I would always dread lockdowns and night times. I dreaded those times in particular because it seemed as if my cell mate would always wait until it was lockdown in order to use the toilet. And I can honestly say I didn't do the same to him; I tried to control myself until after lockdown had ended. Just imagine being locked up with someone who had just gone into a bathroom (a very confined space), used the toilet, and released the most unbearable smell. That's what I constantly had to endure!

When that would happen, I would wish I was skinnier so I could squeeze through the cell bars, but that was only wishful thinking. I would try holding my breath, but I could only do that for so long. The next step was to stuff my head under the pillow, but that didn't work either. At times you can't even stand the smell of your own feces, let alone someone else's! It was stinking bondage! (Sorry for being so graphic.)

Is it possible that when some sort of disaster comes into our lives, it could be God's way of being gracious to us? God could have simply killed Manasseh for all the evil and sins in his life. Instead, God caused disastrous trouble and captivity to come upon him that eventually humbled him and caused him to repent—thus God was able to pardon him and show him the vastness of His grace.

I felt like God was punishing me beyond what I could bear, because, like Manasseh, I didn't turn from my unrighteous ways nor heed His warnings. I cried! I prayed—*Lord, please, please have mercy on me and deliver me! Lord, I acknowledge that I've sinned gravely against You and brought disgrace to Your name and Church, and I've also hurt someone tremendously, among others! Father, please…!*

Within a few weeks, which felt like eternity to me, a single cell was opened up, and I was next in line. I was moved to cell number 12. For me, numbers have always been sort of a significant thing. In the case of the first cell, number three, I felt it was a sign of future resurrection from the stench of death and hopelessness. In the case of cell number 12, I felt like God was reaffirming my role in ministry—like Peter who fell into sin, yet was still one of the 12 apostles.

Then the two cells I was placed in after I was sentenced were numbers four and five. The number four signified to me that the Lord was still calling my name, just as He did when Samuel was a little boy. God didn't give up calling after the first, second, or even the third call, but on the fourth call Samuel got it (see 1 Sam. 3). Also, four days after being dead, Lazarus was raised from the dead when Jesus called his name with a loud voice (see John 11:1-44). And finally, the number five because both the words *grace* and *Jesus* are spelt with five letters, and because I've always applied the five letters of grace to the five stones that David took with him to fight Goliath.

I knew that if I called out to God in my trouble, He would hear me according to His promise in Psalm 50:15 that says, *"Call upon Me in the day of trouble; I will deliver you, and you shall glorify Me."* Though my deliverance was not instant, I committed myself to learning from this season of my life. In every trial, I believe God is able and desiring to give us treasures. Also, I purposed in my heart not to waste this momentous opportunity to be the light in a dark place—and I mean a very dark place! I was going to submit myself to God and allow Him to use me in sharing the Gospel to as many inmates as I possibly could.

When we find ourselves in trouble, for the most part, we always just want out—right away, like Manasseh. We tend to become short sighted and introspective rather than taking on a "God-perspective." We don't really stop and say, "OK, God, I'm in a mess and in trouble, but Lord, even in the midst of everything I still love You and want to be Your vessel; use me."

I didn't consider myself more righteous than the other inmates, at least from a human merit standpoint. My sin (crime) was much more serious and detestable than many (probably most) of theirs. However, I knew that I was in a different position from most of them because I am a Christian, a child of God and, therefore, a saint.

Though my sins had placed me in an environment with others who were there because of their own sins, I had the privilege of praying, "Abba Father." I was and still am in covenantal relationship with Almighty God through the blood of Jesus Christ. This is one of the humbling and yet prestigious factors of Christianity.

Even though Manasseh did not have a personal relationship with God, He at least knew about the God of his fathers. Though it's always better to *know* God than just to know *about* God, it's still a start that may one day help lead you in the right direction to know Him for yourself. For some of us, our past and even some of our most recent behaviors are a lot more sinful than those people the Bible would call unbelieving sinners. But we have relational access to His throne of grace and mercy by the blood of Jesus Christ. At the same time, this is never something to be taken for granted or to be misused.

If righteousness and holiness were strictly based on our own good works, many sinners would be able to put a lot of us to shame. But our boast and glory is in the Lord and in His grace toward us that we have received. Repentance is commanded of all, and forgiveness is readily available to all through the cross, but only some choose to accept it.

Even if we feel like we're as sinful as Manasseh, we don't have to continue in our pride and internal condemnation. Just like Manasseh we can turn to God who is ready and willing to forgive a repentant sinner. And should you have to go through some consequences for your sin, don't regard that as meaning that God hasn't forgiven you or doesn't love you anymore. Remember that He's also a God of justice.

When Moses asked the Lord to show him His glory, my understanding is that Moses was asking the Lord to show him who He really was—what He was all about—the weight of His character, goodness, and so forth. The Lord told Moses He would do it, but that he could not see His face because he would die. So the Lord made preparation for Moses to stand in the cleft of a rock. Then He covered his face with His hands, passed by him, and then removed His hands so he would only see His back.

This is what the Lord declared to Moses:

*The LORD, the LORD God, merciful and gracious, longsuf-
fering, and abounding in goodness and truth, keeping mercy
for thousands, forgiving iniquity and transgression and sin,
by no means clearing the guilty, visiting the iniquity of the
fathers upon the children and the children's children to the
third and the fourth generation* (Exodus 34:6-7).

God was declaring to Moses the core of who He truly is,
and in the midst of that core are both justice and grace. God is a
God of love, mercy, and grace, but He is also a God of justice who
cannot and will not overlook sin. The good news is that mercy triumphs over judgment because His grace is greater than our sins,
and He delights in showing mercy. Just like Manasseh, my story
is one of justice and grace in motion.

FINDING GRACE

Another aspect of Manasseh's story that relates to many today
is the way that he ignored all of God's many warnings. Though
God always wants to have mercy and provide a way out if we
repent, so many of us refuse to listen until we face the fury of His
judgment.

Many people don't want anything to do with God when
everything is going their way. They live as if they're God, as if
they're self-sufficient. They think they'll never need a shoulder to
lean on or cry on or a hand to help them up. When they get to the
end of their rope, they just simply "speak another one into existence," or so they think. All it takes, however, is for a few difficult
realities of life to come knocking at their door constantly. Then
they are screaming out with tears to the God they didn't want
anything to do with or maybe didn't even believe in.

When your back's against the wall or you've been knocked down flat, you kind of run out of options. But you can still look up—if you choose to open your spiritual eyes and look for grace. Grace—God's grace—is simply defined as God giving you what you don't deserve and not giving you what you truly deserve. We are never truly deserving of anything good from the Lord (see Rom. 5:6-11).

Though grace is unmerited favor, it is also all encompassing of the blessedness and goodness of God. Paul puts it this way, *"Or do you despise the riches of His goodness, forbearance, and longsuffering, not knowing that the goodness of God leads you to repentance?"* (Rom. 2:4).

All of the goodness of God is available to all people, even to sinners. However, only those who have been reconciled to Him have full access to *all* of these blessings—like relationship, fellowship, and His Spirit living in their hearts.

In His final moments on the cross, Jesus prayed that His Father would forgive those who were crucifying Him (see Luke 23:32-34). That was mercy and grace in motion, for they certainly did not deserve that prayer. When Lazarus died, Jesus was overwhelmed with emotion. Seeing Mary and Martha, His friends, overcome with tears, He too wept and proceeded to show His mercy by raising Lazarus from the dead (see John 11).

If I were to give one of my kidneys to save a rich man's life, and later on find myself in dire need, it would only be fair and reasonable for that man to show me mercy because of what I had done for him—just as it was reasonable for David to show mercy to Jonathan and his family because of what Jonathan had done for him (see 1 Sam. 19:1-17; 20:1-42; 2 Sam. 9).

You may be in a position where you deserve and can expect mercy from someone, but you will never be in the position where you deserve saving, redeeming grace from God. You can't earn God's grace and salvation. To this very day, it remains the greatest and most precious unconditional gift.

Such Were Some of You

Let's look at two contrasting Scriptures on this subject:

He who overcomes shall inherit all things, and I will be his God and he shall be My son. But the cowardly, unbelieving, abominable, murderers, sexually immoral, sorcerers, idolaters, and all liars shall have their part in the lake of fire which burns with fire and brimstone, which is the second death (Revelation 21:7-8).

The sinners listed here, including the unbelievers, are on their way to eternal damnation, and it's not mainly because of the sinful things they have done, but because they rejected the *gift* of grace and forgiveness that could have been theirs. Consider this next Scripture:

Do you not know that the unrighteous will not inherit the kingdom of God? Do not be deceived. Neither fornicators, nor idolaters, nor adulterers, nor homosexuals, nor sodomites, nor thieves, nor covetous, nor drunkards, nor revilers, nor extortioners will inherit the kingdom of God. And such were some of you. But you were washed, but you were sanctified, but you were justified in the name of the Lord Jesus and by the Spirit of our God (1 Corinthians 6:9-11).

The lists of sinners in these two passages are nearly the same, but verse 11 in First Corinthians 8 makes all the difference, *"And* *such **were** some of you...*" Their sin records have been completely wiped clean and considered as things of the past that have been dealt with. *"But **you were washed**, but **you were sanctified**, but **you were justified**."* None of these people, because of their sinful lifestyles or occasional sins, had been placed beyond the grace of God. Another example is found in Manasseh, who committed almost every sin in the book; Scripture would indicate, however, that he is redeemed and is in Heaven in the presence of the Lord.

The apostles themselves also came into the grace of God from unworthy lifestyles. Paul pointed that out to the Ephesians:

> *And you He made alive, who were dead in trespasses and sins, in which **you** once walked according to the course of this world, according to the prince of the power of the air, the spirit who now works in the sons of disobedience, among whom also **we** all once conducted ourselves in the lusts of our flesh, fulfilling the desires of the flesh and of the mind, and were by nature children of wrath, just as the others* (Ephesians 2:1-3).

If we knew about some of the sinful ways of the apostles before Jesus called them, as well as some of the issues they still struggled with afterward, we would probably be surprised. I wish Paul had gone into a little more detail about his struggle when he said,

> *...For what I will to do, that I do not practice; but what I hate, that I do. If, then, I do what I will not to do, I agree with the law that it is good. But now, it is no longer I who do it, but sin that dwells in me. For I know that in me (that is, in my flesh) nothing good dwells; for to will is present with me, but how to perform what is good I do not find. For the good that I will to do, I do not do; but the evil I will not to do, that I practice* (Romans 7:15-19).

Many scholars would like to put Paul on a pedestal, as if he didn't have struggles. They try to say that though he struggled, it wasn't in a sinful way. But such a belief contradicts Paul's own confession, *"the evil I will not to do…"* It wasn't until Paul had the revelation that victory in the Christian life cannot be achieved by personal effort that he truly began walking in victory. It takes dying to self so that Jesus, by the power of the Holy Spirit, can live through us (see Rom. 7:24-8:14; Gal. 2:19-21; 5:16-26). Paul certainly was not a sinless saint, just a redeemed one.

Maybe the apostles were not guilty of the same sins I committed—or of idolatry, witchcraft, and murder like Manasseh was—but the fact is that they all had to deal with sin issues in their lives. To conclude otherwise would be to contradict the very Word of God by saying there were some sinless saints who did not fall short of the glory of God (see Rom. 3:23).

Hope for the Worst of Us

Perhaps some of you who are reading my story are feeling a great sense of unworthiness, shame, and guilt. Do not give up on the amazing grace of Almighty God! Don't accept the lies of the devil that you are beyond the reach of God's outstretched arms of grace. Whatever situation you're in, wherever you find yourself—in prison, on a sick bed, in bondage and affliction in the enemy's camp, in the belly of a "big fish" like Jonah (see Jon. 2:1-10)—God's heart and hands of grace can reach you! If God's grace could reach Manasseh, then I know it can reach you. I double dare you to believe His grace is greater!

If God's grace was not sufficient and greater than our sins and weaknesses, then, when we find ourselves coming up short in varying ways and degrees, we may as well give up on the hope that's found in His grace. We don't have to be great theologians to figure this out; if God can't or won't forgive us, the devil sure can't and won't.

Certainly, I wouldn't like for anyone to misunderstand my point and say, "Well, if Manasseh did all those things and God forgave him, then I'm safe; I'll make things right, repent, and seek forgiveness later." You may not live to see later. Don't presumptuously test God's grace; you may inadvertently test His wrath. Remember, Manasseh's story isn't just one of grace, compassion, and forgiveness, but also one of wrath—justice wrapped up in grace.

The same is true of my story. I can declare like Paul, "...*By the grace of God I am what I am, and His grace toward me was not in vain...*" (1 Cor. 15:10). Look at what Paul wrote just prior to this. He said, "*For I am the least of the apostles, who am not worthy to be called an apostle, because I* [the other side of me] *persecuted the church of God*" (1 Cor. 15:9). He had reasons to feel unworthy, but in God's grace he was able to stand and be counted worthy. Truly God's grace is greater than our greatest sins. I am so thankful that He has redeemed me and that He is continuing to make me more holy.

CHAPTER 5

PETER'S STORY

You May Fall, but Don't Fail

 The steps of a good man are ordered by the LORD, and He delights in his way. Though he fall, he shall not be utterly cast down; for the LORD upholds him with His hand (Psalm 37:23-24).

Before I got into the ministry with Jesus and later became a disciple and an apostle, I was just a simple fisherman. It was while my brother Andrew and I were fishing that Jesus came by one day and called out to us: *"Follow Me, and I will make you fishers of men"* (Matt. 4:19). So we did, and we became deeply immersed in Jesus and His teachings. I was strongly devoted to Him and had a sincere love for Him. But the day I lied and denied Him, my life was forever changed.

Allow me to share a little background to the main point of my story. I must admit, first of all, that we weren't the greatest of fishermen. So when Jesus called us, we thought, *Why not—let's give the fishing a break for a while.* I hadn't given much time to the studying of the Torah because we were too busy fishing all the time. But deep inside there was a longing for something more—something greater and more fulfilling.

As I watched Jesus heal all manner of sickness and disease and rebuke evil spirits, I was in awe! When I heard Him preach the Kingdom of God with power and authority, my heart shook with conviction. Though others were turning away from Him because the teachings were too deep and convicting and sometimes hard to understand, I just could not go back to fishing, as tough as Jesus' teachings were. For His words were the very words of life. Many times we disciples had to go to Jesus and request further understanding of His teachings, especially the parables. But I never did question His power. After all, He came into my own house and healed my mother-in-law right in front my eyes (see Matt. 8:14-15), not to mention all the other great signs and wonders that He performed.

Faith in the Water

One day when we were all in a boat and Jesus was sleeping, there arose a great storm with fearful wind and waves. We feared for our lives and cried out to Jesus to save us! He got up from His sleep and was as calm as can be, as if there was no storm whatsoever. Then on top of that, He had the nerve to ask us, *"Why are you fearful, O you of little faith?"* (Matt. 8:26).

Give me a break, I thought to myself. *Are You blind? Don't You see what's going on and what could potentially happen?* I loved to talk and was a bold and blunt guy, but I wasn't bold enough to say those thoughts out loud. Nonetheless, He stood up and rebuked the winds and the sea, and instantly there was a great calm (see Matt. 8:23-27).

When you know about the power of God yesterday, it will give you a greater base from which to trust in His power for today—kind of like David remembering his defeat of the lions and bears when he went to face Goliath (see 1 Sam. 17:31-37). This was what gave me courage to step out of the boat and walk on the water one night when Jesus bid me to come. If He had power over the troubled wind and waves and was able to walk upon the water, then, I concluded, He could give me power to do the same. Thus I stepped out in faith, looking steadfastly at Jesus, and walked on the water.

Unfortunately, I became fearful and started doubting. I became overwhelmed by the fierceness of the wind and waves and took my eyes off Jesus, the solution, and placed them on the wind and the waves, the situation. That was it. I started sinking and had to cry out, "Lord, save me!" So He reached out His hand and caught me, and said, "*...O you of little faith, why did you doubt?*" (Matt. 14:31).

QUICK TO SPEAK

I was the kind of guy who loved to talk and was quick to respond and react to things, people, and questions. When Jesus asked the disciples, "*Who do men say that I, the Son of Man, am?*" And again, "*Who do you say that I am?*" I blurted it out, "*You are the Christ, the Son of the living God*" (Matt. 16:13-16). I would have liked to take credit for my correct answer, but everything was quickly put into perspective by Jesus, who said, "*...flesh and blood has not revealed this to you, but My Father who is in heaven*" (Matt. 16:17).

But being quick to answer was not always to my advantage. Not long after, when I learned that Jesus was going to suffer many things from the elders, chief priests, and scribes and eventually be killed, I took Him aside and rebuked Him! "*Far be it from You,*

Lord; this shall not happen to You!" (Matt. 16:22). But then to my surprise, Jesus turned and said to me, *"...Get behind Me, Satan! You are an offense to Me, for you are not mindful of the things of God, but the things of men"* (Matt. 16:23).

Was He calling me "satan"? No, He wasn't. He was rebuking the devil who spoke through me. The Peter through whom God had just spoken was the same Peter through whom satan spoke too. Through this I learned that I could be God's vessel and oracle as well as I could be satan's vessel and oracle. I had a choice to make. Whose words would I speak?

THE SERVANT

I was anointed along with the other disciples to go out and cure diseases, heal the sick, cast out demons, raise the dead, and preach the Gospel of the Kingdom (see Luke 9:1-6). Demons were subject to us in Jesus' name. I saw Jesus transfigured on the mountain (see Luke 9:28-36); heard the Sermon on the Mount (see Matt. 5–7); participated in the feeding of the 5,000 (see Matt. 14:13-21); and witnessed the raising of Lazarus from the dead (see John 11); and the healing of the woman with the issue of blood (see Luke 8:40-48). I was there for it all. And I thought I knew Him and loved Him best.

When, during our Passover meal, Jesus started preparing to wash my feet, I said, *"You shall never wash my feet!"* (John 13:8). I thought that was the job of a servant, and Jesus was my master. I should be washing His feet. I just didn't get it—plain and simple. I didn't understand what it symbolized and the significance of it. So when Jesus corrected me, and I learned what it meant, I submitted myself to His will.

Everything was going alright up until this point. Then Jesus made it very clear that He was about to be betrayed and killed. This was not good. Suddenly, there arose a dispute among the 12 of us as to who was going to betray Him. My love for Jesus was questioned, and I questioned the love of others for Jesus. Then someone asked, "Who is the greatest?"

I thought I was the greatest because I've always been the spokesman—the bold one. But John and James had reasons to state their claim too, and so did all the rest. It became a major dispute. Jesus did not intervene immediately because His heart was heavy and deeply concerned with what was about to happen. But He finally set us all straight: *"…He who is greatest among you, let him be as the younger* [servant]*…"* (Luke 22:26).

I didn't know what was coming my way or what was going on behind the scenes as Jesus drew closer to His sufferings. While I was there arguing about who was going to betray Him and who was the greatest among us, satan was plotting my destruction.

SIFTED BY THE ENEMY

Jesus looked me in the eye with compassion and fervent love and said,

Simon, Simon! Indeed, Satan has asked for you, that he may sift you as wheat. But I have prayed for you, that your faith should not fail; and when you have returned to Me, strengthen your brethren (Luke 22:31-32).

At the time, I didn't fully grasp what Jesus was saying. I briefly thought of the story of Job, but then I shook myself back to my ego and replied, *"Lord, I am ready to go with You, both to prison and to death"* (Luke 22:33). Jesus was quick to point out the deception of the human heart—that I didn't know myself as much as I thought I did. He told me the rooster would not crow before I denied Him three times (see Luke 22:34). I didn't know what to think or say next, so I left it at that.

That very same night we all, except for Judas, went to the Mount of Olives, to the Garden of Gethsemane, as was our custom. Jesus took me, James, and John together away from the rest. Before long, He started to pour out His soul, which was filled with distress; He was exceedingly sorrowful! So He told us to pray that we might not enter into temptation while He went off a short distance to pray by Himself (see Matt. 26:36-41).

We were very tired and sorrowful, as He was, and though we tried to pray, we all fell asleep. Three times He came back and found us sleeping and was very displeased. The third time would be the last. While Jesus was still speaking to us, a crowd of temple guards and some priests came by and arrested Him. Judas, the betrayer, was also with them and kissed Jesus as a way of indentifying Him (see Matt. 26:44-51).

When they drew near to arrest Jesus, I drew my sword to kill one of the high priest's servants, but he ducked and my sword cut off his ear. Jesus again rebuked me because He was about to culminate His mission on the cross and I was trying to stop Him (see John 18:10-11).

So they took Jesus away to the high priest's house, and I followed at a distance. A servant girl came by while I was warming myself at the fire in the courtyard, and she said, *"This man was also with Him"* (Luke 22:56). I replied, *"Woman, I do not know Him"* (Luke 22:57). Later, another saw me and began telling those who stood by that I was one of the disciples, but I denied it and told them I didn't know Him (see Luke 22:58).

Then about an hour later, I was confronted again and accused of being one of Jesus' disciples, and for the third time I denied it: *"Man, I do not know what you are saying"* (Luke 22:60). I became angry and began to swear and curse. I thought, maybe if I started swearing and cursing they would really believe me because Jesus' disciples didn't talk like that.

Meanwhile, my heart was being torn in two! I wanted to associate with Jesus, but I wasn't sure what would happen. I didn't want to die. When I denied Him the third time, I heard the rooster crow. And, if that wasn't heart-piercing enough, Jesus turned and looked me right in the face. Then I remembered everything He had said to me. It was the most excruciating pain I've ever felt! I went away and wept bitterly for hours (see Luke 22:60-62). My love and commitment were not as strong as I thought they were—circumstances had proven it.

I watched from a distance as Jesus stood before the high priests and Pilate, and I heard all the accusations they brought against Him. I knew they were all lies, but who was I to confront them and say, "You're lying," when I had just told the three biggest lies in the whole Scripture!

It's one thing if you lie for or against your friend or a spiritual or biological brother, but to lie and deny that you know Jesus is one of the most regrettable things you could ever do. People may turn their backs on others, including family members, and still be saved, but they cannot turn their backs on the only one who can save them and still be saved—that is, if they fail to return to Him in repentance.

I watched as they released a renegade and a murderer instead of Jesus and then pronounced the judgment of crucifixion on Him (see Luke 23:1-25). *Would things have turned out differently if I had not denied Him and turned my back on Him? Would they have killed me instead as an example and a threat to Jesus to stop His ministry?* These were some of the thoughts going through my mind.

It was heart-wrenching to say the least! Some of the same people who had eaten from Jesus' hand, who had seen His miraculous power, and who had proclaimed, *"Hosanna to the Son of David! Blessed is He who comes in the name of the LORD! Hosanna in the highest"* (Matt. 21:9), were now saying, *"Crucify Him"* (Luke 23:21).

Even though I wanted to be angry at them, I knew my anger could not be justified, considering what I had just done to Him. Though all of this betrayal from the people must have been very hurtful to Jesus, I thought to myself that my denial of Him must have hurt even more. I was His close friend—a disciple. The wound of a close friend is deeper than that of an associate. It's the close friend who knows your weaknesses, your strengths, your secrets, and your vulnerability—the person of acquaintance normally doesn't. The friend who is closest is the one who can stab you in the back the worst—just as Judas did to Jesus, as Delilah did to Samson, and as I did to Jesus. No, I didn't stab Him in the back with betrayal, but my denial was just as painful and penetrating.

When the Romans were scourging Him and crucifying Him, I cried until my eyes were dry! And even then, my heart was still in tears. I remembered asking Jesus, *"How often shall my brother sin against me, and I forgive him? Up to seven times?"* And He had replied and said to me, *"...up to seventy times seven"* (Matt. 18:21-22). That's 490 times! But of course, that number is not a cap on forgiveness. Jesus gave this big estimate because it's unlikely that we would need to forgive someone that many times. Jesus was telling me how expansive and far reaching my willingness and obedience to forgive others must be. As I recalled what Jesus had said, I figured He would live what He preached and forgive me. But even if He would forgive me, I didn't know if I could forgive myself.

I remembered so well when Jesus told me that satan was seeking my demise and failure and that I would indeed fall, but eventually be restored. And He had said He prayed for me! It was His grace that kept me. Between me and suicide were His prayer and His hand of grace. I'm not saying I was suicidal, but I could have been. People kill themselves for much less than that. I denied Him, but was kept by Him. Judas, on the other hand, betrayed Him and hanged himself (see Matt. 27:3-5). I don't know what would've happened if it were not for His gracious prayer over me—I just don't know.

Despite having confidence about my future destiny, I was beating up myself in the present. As I recalled certain teachings of Jesus, my spirit became feeble within me. Jesus had said, *"Whoever confesses Me before men, him the Son of Man also will confess before the angels of God. But he who denies Me before men will be denied before the angels of God"* (Luke 12:8-9). I had to believe in the unconditional love and grace of Christ, that He was able to look beyond my faults and see my need. Considering the fact that He had said to me, *"When you have returned to Me* [are converted], *strengthen your brethren"* (Luke 22:32), I had faith that He would forgive me and that I would be reconciled to Him. Either I was going to believe and live—rise again, or I was going to doubt and die—fall and fail.

FORGIVENESS AND REINSTATEMENT

When I heard that Jesus had risen from the dead, I did not believe it. So I ran to the tomb to see for myself, but John outran me. It wasn't that I couldn't run faster than John, but my denial of Him was still haunting me, and I didn't know what to expect when He would look me in the face—again. I felt like a betrayer, a liar, and a failure. When we got to the tomb, He was not there. So we went back to the house with a heavy, troubled, and confused hearts.

We had heard He was alive from Mary Magdalene, Mary the mother of James, and Salome, who had taken spices to the tomb of Jesus. There they encountered an angel and saw that the stone was rolled away from the tomb. The angel, while talking to them, singled me out, indicating that I was still considered a disciple. The angel said to them,

> *Do not be alarmed. You seek Jesus of Nazareth, who was crucified. He is risen! He is not here. See the place where they laid Him. But go, tell His disciples—and Peter—that He is going before you into Galilee; there you will see Him...* (Mark 16:6-7).

This was God's doing. He wanted to reassure me personally that He still loved me, still considered me a saint, a disciple, and a part of the family. He was telling me that if I was feeling a sense of condemnation and failure, I needed to dispose of those feelings and return to Him just as He had taught us in the story of the prodigal son (see Luke 15:11-32). So though I felt nervous about seeing Jesus again, I was also sure He had forgiven me.

Later that day when we were together in the house, while the door was shut, Jesus appeared out of nowhere! And He said to us,

"Peace be with you" (John 20:19-20). There was a look of grace and glory on His face! I was waiting for Him to confront me about how I denied Him, but He never mentioned it. I could not believe my eyes or my ears! However, a few days later Jesus came to me and asked me a question—the same question three times, *"...Do you love Me more than these...?"* (John 21:15-17). I was hurt and became angry that He was questioning my love for Him! Was it because I had denied Him three times that He was now questioning my love for Him three times? That's how I felt. Each time I gave Him my answer, saying that I did love Him, He commissioned me to feed His sheep and to feed His lambs.

GROWING UP IN HIM

Jesus pardoned me, and I was never the same. After I received the infilling of the Holy Spirit, along with the rest who were gathered in the upper room on the Day of Pentecost, I was filled with supernatural boldness and a deeper commitment to Jesus and the Kingdom of God (see Acts 4:8-20). I boldly began proclaiming salvation in Jesus' name and my allegiance to Him. I didn't have any second thoughts about publicly proclaiming the Gospel, even when I knew my life and well-being were in danger.

As a matter of fact, John and I were personally threatened not to preach in Jesus' name anymore (see Acts 4:1-24). But we did not shy away from persecution because we all wanted to finish the race that we were called to run, and that race included persecutions.

We experienced it all, just as Paul put it:

We are hard-pressed on every side, yet not crushed; we are perplexed but not in despair; persecuted, but not forsaken; struck down, but not destroyed—always carrying about in the body the dying of the Lord Jesus, that the life of Jesus also may be manifested in our body (2 Corinthians 4:8-10).

The transformation in my life was truly incredible. I went from being a fearful and faithless denier of Jesus to a bold and faithful witness—all because of His saving and sanctifying power! There are many other stories that I could tell. For more on my life, read the Gospels, the Book of Acts, and the two epistles that bear my name.

Ray's Reflections and Insights

When I had sinned so disgracefully and was in jail, I knew for a fact, based on the Word of God, that my sins were not beyond the power of His redeeming blood—though some of the saints made it seem that way. I understood that if I sincerely, with godly sorrow, confessed my sins and repented, the Lord would forgive me just like He forgave Peter. Unfortunately, I wrestled with forgiving myself!

Every so often my mind would take me back to the event, and all the "could haves" and "should haves" would begin to bombard my mind. I started asking myself questions like, *Why did I...? How could I...? Where did I go wrong? Why didn't I...? What was I thinking?* This was a mental prison! In this kind of prison, which many people find themselves in, there is almost no release, and most definitely there can be no "prison breaks" from within. There can only be a deliverer—a Savior. (Of course, there are other things that can keep peoples' souls in prison that are not sin related.)

Then all at once my eyes were opened to the words of Isaiah the prophet when he declared, concerning Jesus,

The Spirit of the Lord GOD is upon Me, because the LORD has anointed Me to preach good tidings to the poor; He has sent Me to heal the brokenhearted, to proclaim liberty to the captives, and the opening of the prison to those who are bound (Isaiah 61:1).

There was no relief, nowhere to run or hide. The only hope I had was Jesus and the Word of Almighty God.

For as the heavens are high above the earth, so great is His mercy toward those who fear Him…As a father pities his children, so the LORD pities those who fear Him (Psalm 103:11-13).

"You may fall, but don't fail" was the kind of motto I took on. In my spiritual battle, I would declare to the enemy of my soul,

Do not rejoice over me, my enemy; when I fall, I will arise; when I sit in darkness, the LORD will be a light to me. I will bear the indignation of the LORD, because I have sinned against Him, until He pleads my case and executes justice for me. He will bring me forth to the light; I will see His righteousness (Micah 7:8-9).

Either I was going to believe the Lord, take Him at His Word, declare it from my heart and mouth, and be set free from my prison, or I was going to refuse to believe and remain in my prison. I had to choose. And I chose life—freedom. I was not going to believe in my feelings above the eternal and unchanging Word of God. Though Peter struggled with his denial of Christ, I believe there was a part of him that still held on to the words of falling and getting back up that Jesus had prophesied over him. I had to get back up like Peter. Yes, I was still in a physical prison, but most importantly, my soul was set free, and I was strengthened and reconciled in my walk with the Lord—first things first.

GRIEF FOR MY VICTIM

One of the most difficult things was the thought and reality of what my victim must be going through. Though I couldn't sleep at night, I figured it had to be twice as difficult for my victim.

In Peter's case, his weakness didn't just hurt or affect Jesus; I'm sure Mary the mother of Jesus was hurt too—especially if she was in the vicinity to hear Peter's denial of her Son. Jesus was a victim of Peter's lies. And I do believe Peter didn't just grieve over the fact that he fell; but also over what Jesus was going through and the toll it took on His mother, among others.

You see, even though my experience was hurtful and I was crying out to God for grace, I had settled in my spirit that I deserved the punishment that was being inflicted. As a matter of fact, I was spared even greater punishment, but had I experienced it all, even then it would have been just.

But my victim most definitely did not deserve the pain, trauma, and scars she had to deal with, possibly for the rest of her life! I was helpless in that regard. A letter of apology might only bring back memories and make things worse—not to mention that I was forbidden to make any direct or indirect communication with the victim. So I prayed for her. I got down on my knees on the cold concrete floor of my jail cell, time and time again, and prayed for her!

I prayed that God would help her, comfort her, strengthen her, heal her, and surround her with His assuring presence. I prayed that the devil would not be allowed to take any advantage of the hurt and trauma that she had experienced at my hands. I prayed that God would remove any nightmares from her dreams and give her beautiful and wonderful dreams. My heart was sincere, and I prayed that God would help her in her own context, even as I was seeking His help in mine.

HOPE FOR THE FUTURE

At my psychiatric evaluation, which was followed up by counseling, they told me that once a person goes down the crime road, it's easier to go down that road again. I certainly respected those psychiatrists for their in-depth knowledge and understanding of the workings and behavior of the human species and our brains— plus the sincere effort and study it took to legitimize them in their profession. However, I personally didn't take such assessments as absolute truth.

Peter himself was faced with other opportunities wherein he could have run, denied Jesus again, and saved himself some tribulation (see Acts 4:1-22; 5:17-42). Peter's initial fall did not make it easier for him to fall again in like manner. If anything, that weakness made him stronger to not fall in the same rut again.

Some may conclude that I'm a danger and a risk to society. We are all free to make our own assumptions, "guess-timations," and assessments regarding anything, and in that regard, I might not be able to do much to alleviate someone's feeling or concern toward me. Nevertheless, I hope that others will give me the benefit of the doubt in my commitment to bearing fruits worthy of repentance (see Matt. 3:8). And this is not to say by any means that I'll never fall again. I believe I'm truly sincere about my remorse and my determination never to reoffend in any way similar to my fall of the past.

Because I know the forgiveness and love of Christ, I have been freed from self-hatred, which is something that any convict with a conscience struggles with. Perhaps that is why so many return to a life of crime; they believe that's just who they are and that there's no hope for them. Regardless, I do not hate myself or despise my freedom enough to return to that lifestyle. Certainly I am not fascinated with prison or the experience of having people, namely guards, treat me like a write-off from humanity.

Considering the deep hurt that my actions caused my victim, her family and friends, my family and friends, and even society as a whole—the displeasure, discomfort, and even anger—plus what I've been through and am still going through, I refuse to be another negative reoffender statistic!

Peter wasn't numb to the fact that he caused deep hurt to Jesus because of his denial. I believe Peter purposed in his heart that, even though he may still fall, he would never again deny a friend, especially Jesus.

I've messed up my life enough, and I don't intend to spend the rest of my days creating anymore mess. But I do intend to make the best out of what is left as I channel the negatives of my past into a positive future. I know with God it's possible. I must dream again, believe again, and get back up again because I'm not yet at the end.

ABANDONMENT

My experience of abandonment is not unique to my situation, but the reality of saints abandoning each other happens all too often. Fellow saints aren't just being abandoned because of their sin, but also in the midst of personal problems and difficult struggles or troubles. In this chapter, as we have seen, Peter wasn't the one who was abandoned by others; he was the one who did the abandonment. Paul, on the other hand, knew what it was like to be abandoned in a time of need. He would have liked to see a few brethren supporting him and standing with him through his trials, but they were nowhere to be found. Paul stated,

> *At my first defense no one stood with me, but all forsook me. May it not be charged against them. But the Lord stood with me and strengthened me, so that the message might be preached fully through me...* (2 Timothy 4:16-17).

Though Paul alluded to the reassuring presence of the Lord, I'm sure he would have appreciated the tangible comfort of his brothers and sisters. Yes, God comforts our spirits, souls, and bodies, but sometimes He knows that we really need a literal embrace and someone to share with face-to-face. I know how just receiving a loving and encouraging letter in prison uplifted my spirit and morale!

I have never heard of someone who was physically embraced by the Lord. God may not literally stretch down His arms from Heaven to embrace us, but He'll do it, as He does with so many other things, indirectly through others. This is why Jesus said, "... *inasmuch as you did it to one of the least of these My brethren, you did it to Me*" (Matt. 25:40). Community is so important in the Body of Christ. He has called us to be His hands and feet to our hurting and needy brothers and sisters.

EVEN IF YOU FALL, DON'T FAIL

One thing I really like about Peter, though some may see it as a flaw, was his willingness to take a risk, even if he ended up failing. Many may look down on Peter because, when he was walking on water, he doubted and sank, but we must remember that he had the guts to step out of the boat in the first place. It seems like it's always so much easier to focus on other people's negatives before taking note of the positives—if we do at all. In the Kingdom, it should be the reverse. We should be quick to see the fingerprints of God in other people—the ways that they're succeeding—and slow to notice their shortcomings. A great example of this is seen in how the Lord addresses the churches in the Book of Revelation chapters 2 and 3.

Many people haven't stumbled at anything, but it's because they haven't tried anything. The man who tries and comes up short is wiser than the man who hasn't tried at all because the one who came short will at least know what doesn't work, and the lessons he learned from his shortcomings will aid him in his next attempt. Better yet, the smarter person will learn from the mistakes of others and save himself the trouble.

Peter certainly learned from his mistakes. And he used those lessons, by the grace of the Holy Spirit, to overcome his weaknesses and to excel in the very area (boldness in standing for Christ) in which he had previously failed his Lord.

The point of Peter's story (and I hope mine) is: You may fall, but you don't have to fail. When Jesus called Peter in His omniscient (all-knowing) knowledge, He knew Peter was going to stumble and fall. In fact, He even told Peter about it. The fullness of the purpose for which He called Peter was not in whether he would pass the test and not deny Him at His ordeal leading up to His crucifixion, but rather in whether Peter would fulfill his purpose and complete his race. If his purpose had been to not deny Christ, he would not have fulfilled it. He fell and would have failed altogether. But Peter's purpose was bigger than that.

Let's look at David's example as well. The Scriptures say, *"David, after he had served his own generation by the will of God, fell asleep, was buried with his fathers..."* (Acts 13:36). Not only does it say that he lived *"by the will of God,"* but the Scriptures even used David as a marker to categorize how the kings after him lived (see 1 Kings 11:38; 15:3,11; 2 Kings 14:3). David fulfilled God's purpose for his life, but he did not achieve it without falling. As we know, he fell miserably. The believers' race is not a sprint, but a marathon.

If a man trips and falls in a sprint, it is next to impossible for him to get back up and win the race. But the race of life is not a sprint. Paul puts it this way, *"I have fought the good fight, I have finished the race, I have kept the faith. Finally, there is laid up for me the crown of righteousness..."* (2 Tim. 4:7-8).

In a marathon, if a man falls, it is more than possible for him to get back up and still win the race. In this talk of racing, we must remember that we are not competing against each other in a race where there is only one winner or a tie for first place and everybody else is a loser. We are competing against ourselves. Each of us must run our own race and fulfill the purpose God has for us. We need not compete with anybody else, but just run our own race and—most importantly—finish well!

RUN WITH FAITH

The significance of unwavering faith is paramount for the believer; that's why Jesus prayed that Peter's faith would not fail. He didn't pray that his kindness, self-control, joy, boldness, discipline, preaching, strength, and so forth would not fail. He prayed for his faith. All these other things are great and should remain in the believer, but when push comes to shove and the rubber really hits the road, it's our faith or lack of it that will help to either make or break us.

Hebrews 11:6 says, *"But without faith it is impossible to please Him, for he who comes to God must believe that He is, and that He is a rewarder of those who diligently seek Him."* The righteous are called to live and walk by faith.

Of all the armor that Paul mentioned for the believer, he said, *"...**above all,** taking the shield of faith with which you will be able to quench all the fiery darts of the wicked one"* (Eph. 6:16). He gave special emphasis to the shield—to faith.

When we fall and find ourselves in a valley, the devil starts shooting feelings of fear, failure, shame, guilt, and condemnation; it's the shield of faith that will be both our defensive and offensive protection at the same time. We can quote Scripture all we want and wield the sword of the Spirit, which is the Word of God (see Eph. 6:17), from Genesis to Revelation, but if we don't apply faith and declare it by faith, we will not have victory. None of the armaments that Paul mentioned are physical; they are spiritual. They're a belief system that is applied by faith and used by faith.

Consider, for example, that the only thing the children of Israel had to hold on to during their 430 years of slavery in Egypt was faith—faith in God and the promise He made to their forefathers. Like the Israelites, Peter had to hold on to the words Jesus had spoken over his life. Jesus had informed Peter that he would fall, but He also reassured him that he would not fail. The same was true for me.

FIGHTING A GOOD FIGHT

God, though He knows all things according to His omniscient power, forgives based on the present. If a saint who committed murder today was serving time in prison and, from a broken heart and contrite spirit with all sincerity and repentance, asked the Lord to forgive him, He would. God will pardon that saint even if He knows that 20 years down the road that saint will again commit murder.

God does not withhold forgiveness from sinners who are seeking saving grace to be born again, nor from saints who sin, even if He knows that they'll be back tomorrow asking for forgiveness again for the same thing. How many of us, for example, have ever only lied once? Jeremiah in the Book of Lamentations said, *"Through the LORD's mercies we are not consumed, because His compassions fail not. They are new every morning; great is Your faithfulness"* (Lam. 3:22-23).

I like to compare my story and even that of Peter to a boxing match. A fighter may get knocked down in the first, second, or even eleventh round and still come back and win the match. If the opponent knocks him down, it doesn't mean that he has lost the match and that he's a failure; he just lost that fight—that round. The objective of the match is not necessarily who can knock down the other person first, even though that can be helpful in declaring the ultimate winner. If being knocked down was the identifying sign of a failure, many great boxers would have lost a match that later on proved them to be champions. Many would have fallen, never to rise again with another chance—including me.

The objective of the match, however, is to either knock your opponent out so he's not able to continue—or to remain strong in the fight to the last bell, with the hope of out-scoring your opponent in points. You're a failure if you get knocked down in your life and you refuse to get back up and overcome like the overcomer the Lord said you are in Him. Tell the devil, "It's not over till God says it's over!" He may win the fight in a particular round, but by the grace of God, he won't win the match! He may win a battle, but don't let him win the war!

I want to encourage those who have experienced heartbreaking setbacks and are struggling with getting back on their feet to finish their course. The Lord does not mark you off when you fall, even though others may. Do you want to know the truth? He comes down even lower in order to pick you up so you won't fail, but win.

CHAPTER 6

RAY'S STORY, PART 2

Hitting the Bottom of Rock Bottom

 ...If I make my bed in hell, behold, You are there. If I take the wings of the morning, and dwell in the uttermost parts of the sea, even there Your hand shall lead me, and Your right hand shall hold me. If I say, "Surely the darkness shall fall on me," even the night shall be light about me (Psalm 139:8-11).

A few days before my jail experience began, I had a dream. In this dream, I was framed by someone, which resulted in me being shot and killed by the police. Immediately my spirit was soaring through the heavens and landed at a destination that was not familiar to me. It was not hell, nor was it Heaven. Then mysteriously, my spirit turned aside and looked a short distance away, and there I was, my skeleton lying on the ground. That's when it dawned on me that I was truly dead. I immediately began crying out to God, "Lord, please have mercy on me! I haven't accomplished all your plans for my life…I haven't fulfilled my purpose yet!" No sooner than I was finished, I heard the voice of the Lord say to me, "I have a mission for you."

For God to have a mission for me, and for me to carry it out, He would have to raise me up from this state of death. This resurrection, however, was yet in the future. I was now about to experience the death of my dream—hitting the bottom of rock bottom.

ALONE IN MY STRUGGLE

I was struggling, struggling with pornography. It wasn't a lifelong struggle, even though I had been exposed to it at about the age of 13. I had been free for years, but then it all came back, and I found myself trapped! These chains of bondage were sucking the life out of me! Little did I know that satisfying the pleasure of my eyes was really slow-motion suicide. It was draining me and leaving me dry.

Maybe if I'd sought help, regardless of how I thought others/leaders would react, things would have been different. And informing my wife as a way of seeking her help wasn't keeping me accountable either; because for whatever reason I thought I could conquer this issue on my own. So though I was alone in my struggle, I had no one to blame but me, myself, and I.

Unfortunately, the Church has often had an unspoken taboo against admitting that we're being tempted in certain areas, as if being tempted is a sign of weakness and sin. But Jesus was tempted; all of us are, though obviously in different areas. This idea that we can't let anyone know we're being tempted in a certain area because of what they might think about us is very dangerous. Even more unfortunate is that this kind of thinking is sometimes based in reality because, rather than getting the help and support you need, you are often judged with a "holier than thou" attitude. This stops people who truly need help in overcoming their struggles. There is no help for those who won't admit they have a problem.

SEXUAL TEMPTATION

God does not take away our sexual impulse when we become born again or when we experience the baptism of the Holy Spirit. However, self-control is one of the fruit of the Spirit that is made readily available to believers to help us walk in sanctification (see Gal. 5:22-23). Paul said, *"I discipline my body and bring it into subjection, lest, when I have preached to others, I myself should become disqualified"* (1 Cor. 9:27). It won't just happen automatically overnight; it's a daily discipline and dependence upon God. This does not just apply to sexual temptations, but to all other areas where we might be tempted to sin.

Men are stimulated primarily by sight and, therefore, have to be on guard at all times to let sight just be sight—to not let it go to the next level, lust. It's becoming more and more evident that a shocking percentage of Christian brothers, and even sisters, are struggling with pornography within the Church.[1] Not many want to really talk about such a sensitive secret sin, but I will attempt to reveal this mountain of sin for what it is and to make others aware of its subtle yet obvious destructive power.

I'll get to my story in a bit, but let me address this issue for a moment. I've seen in my own life how it makes you live in secrecy and darkness while trying to cover up your tracks. It's the bondage that'll keep you longer than you want to stay, take you farther than you want to go, keep you in darkness when your soul is crying out for light, make you cry out in frustration when you should be shouting in celebration, and cost you more than you want to pay. I've heard testimonies of how it destroyed marriages and families, cost people their jobs, their integrity, and on and on. It will devour your love and leave you with lust. It will devour your sincerity and leave you with hypocrisy. The spirit behind it is merciless and could care less about your happiness.

The world's view of Christians as hypocrites is not entirely unfounded, though it's a partial truth with a general stereotype of the saints. A lot of us don't want to say anything to anyone when we're struggling with issues, especially sin issues, because there are pros and cons to being open and honest. Sunday after Sunday, many of us dress from head to toe in the most adorable outfits, but on the inside we're ugly and naked—miserable and not at peace with ourselves because we know in our heart of hearts that all is not well. We have learned how to shout when we're living in doubt, how to dance while we live by chance, how to praise while we gaze, how to worship while we gossip, how to sing while we sin, and so forth.

If you can bear witness to what I'm saying, then great; keep reading. If not, then great; keep reading too. Please understand, I'm preaching first and foremost to myself. My goal is not to cast stones at others who, in fact, may be more righteous than I am. As I discuss some flaws in the Church, know that I am not blind to the role I have played in all of this.

THE POWER OF ADDICTION

Pornography can never fulfill anyone. It only satisfies you for the moment, but shortly afterward leaves you with an even deeper craving for more. The more images you see, the more images you want to see. It's a trap. I didn't want it in my life, and if there had been a button that I could have just pressed to be completely free from it, I would not have hesitated to do so. But it wasn't that easy. You may not understand if you've never been an addict before, but not everybody who is addicted to something wants to remain that way. And freedom is not necessarily a matter of will power either. If it was, Paul would never have written Romans chapter 7, and many addicts who sincerely want to be free would just break themselves free and forget A.A.

Some try to sound super-spiritual and say, "If you really wanted to be free, you would be free. You didn't want to be free because you enjoyed it." Though this may be true of some, it is an oversimplification that Romans 7 clearly contradicts. The apostle Paul was a mature believer who certainly would have pushed the "get free" button had one existed. Yet it's clear that whatever struggles or strongholds he was facing, he wanted sincerely to be free from them (to stop doing them), but he found himself bound to them. Some may reason that it wasn't an addiction issue, but when I read Romans 7, it seems to be very plain to me that he was a slave to his struggles or habits. His use of the word *evil* indicates to me that it was real addiction and bondage.

If you have never been addicted, especially to something that's negative and destructive, maybe you won't really understand— and, therefore, you may not be as considerate of others who are addicted. When people are going outside in below-freezing temperatures just to have a smoke, while they're shivering from head to toe, you know that's an addiction—and one that is not so easy to be free from. The person who really wants to quit smoking still goes out in the cold to smoke. People may think, *If they really want to quit, shouldn't the cold be enough to deter them?* It should be, but it isn't. That's the nature of addiction. It destroys the ability to make logical decisions in the area of addiction, even when the addict really wants to do the right thing.

I remember watching Gospel singer and musician, Kirk Franklin, on the *Oprah Show* confessing how he used to be in bondage to pornography, but sincerely wanted to quit. He even confessed that he would throw away the video in the garbage bin, but found himself in the dark going back out to the garbage bin to dig through the garbage in order to retrieve the video. No he wasn't a mad man looking for food in the garbage; he was sane, but addicted and in bondage, and it was that bondage that pulled him back to the garbage. But praise God, Kirk also testified of his deliverance to finally walk in the freedom by which Christ has made us free (see Gal. 5:1).

Pornography was my worst nightmare. I wondered how different and pure (or purer) my life would have been if I had not been exposed to it. I wonder if a part of the devil's plan is to present different activities and practices to people, some of which might not even be sinful, in hopes that they will be so engrossed in them that they eventually become habit. Later, for those who become Christians, the enemy brings back these old habits to hinder them from getting closer to God—kind of like a dog returning to its vomit.

This is why many people who, for example, drank alcohol on a regular basis or were alcoholics before they got saved are often tempted with the same thing they enjoyed before they got saved. They are more likely to fall for it than for something that they were never addicted to previously. There was nothing good about slavery in Egypt, but many times along the Israelites' journey, especially when things got tough and looked discouraging, they were ready to go back to Egypt—to slavery (see Num. 14:1-4). It's sad, but it's true.

THE BITTER FRUIT OF PORNOGRAPHY

I found out that if you're married, which I was, pornography will make you feel dissatisfied no matter how great your sex life is or how sexy/handsome your wife or husband is. The hidden agenda in pornography is not to satisfy you, but to make you dissatisfied. It always puts curious fantasies in your mind and makes you want to explore and experience different "adventures." It takes away your sleep and gives you a false energy that will make you stay up for hours looking at images. Then, when it's time to go to work, you become a walking sleeping man because the false energy of the enemy's deception is gone and leaves you hanging—a workplace safety hazard. The joy of the Lord will most certainly not be your strength then (see Neh. 8:10)! And of course, the devil who entices you to sin is the same devil who turns around and condemns you after the act.

FREEDOM FROM BONDAGE

Today I am free from the bondage of pornography through the power of God, and I am walking in victory by daily yielding to the Spirit of God instead of the temptation. I would love to be able to say to those who are struggling, "Do this and that and memorize such and such a Scripture to declare over your life every day, and you too will be free."

Unfortunately, there is no one-step-fits-all application for how and when one may be set free. Some have experienced instantaneous deliverance, while for others it's been gradual. There are, however, a few things that I personally believe need to happen.

First, you must want and need to be set free. Second, you must surrender to the Spirit of God and start becoming a doer of the Word (see James 1:22-25). Third, you must involve an accountability partner or an accountability Website like covenanteyes. com. Fourth, you will most certainly need the anointing power of the Holy Spirit to break the yoke. Finding freedom requires spiritual disciplines and the establishment of boundaries. It's not easy, but it's possible. Christ came and died to set captives free.

My Personal Battle

Before I convey the details of my crime, I want to warn you that what you read may deeply disturb or offend you. I do not seek to be an insensitive writer, but neither do I want to sugarcoat or omit my story. Please proceed with caution. I do hope, more than anything else, that you will get the message behind my messy story. After all, it would not be satisfying and beneficial to me or anyone if, at the end of this book, you go away with the mess of my story and leave the message.

O Lord, please strengthen me if You want me to share this shameful and hurtful part of my story! Lord, the memory of it hurts me! And even as I'm writing, You can see how much I'm shivering and hesitant to go on! But in the mighty name of Jesus Christ, I receive Your strength, even right now! I would not be sharing my story, making myself vulnerable, and exposing the other side of me more than it's already been exposed, if You had not told me to share it. So because You told me to do it, I know You'll grant me Your grace that will enable me to do it. In Jesus' name, I pray. Amen.

In the process of time, I got laid off from my job and became a bit depressed about it. This gave me an even more undesirable opportunity of time to feed the pornographic cravings. The internal battle was raging. Even though I wanted to stop and I cried out to the Lord to help me, I found myself doing the very thing I didn't want to. I found myself in a situation where my spirit was ready and willing to walk in holiness, but my flesh was weak and wanted to please itself with sinful pleasure.

One day a thought came into my mind of how to go about giving birth (fulfillment) to one of the desires (fantasies) that had been conceived in me. So I pondered and wrestled with the idea for a few days. Then one night, I decided to stay up late in order to execute my plan. I got an old shirt to make a mask to cover my face, a dress tie to use for blindfolding the victim, tape for restraining, and a knife just in case I needed it to help open the window. Off I went in the middle of the night to break into my friend's apartment. On my way to her place, and even before I left my apartment, the Holy Spirit kept on saying, "Ray, don't do it. Don't go." But I ignored His voice. Since the desire and thought had already been conceived in me, and I wasn't yielding my will to the Holy Spirit to perform spiritual abortion, I was inevitably on my way to give birth to sin—the desire (see James 1:13-15).

What was ironic about this ordeal is that I was in the process of writing a book titled *Spiritual Abortion*. Obviously, I needed to deal with me first before I started going around trying to tell people how to perform spiritual abortion and what can happen if and when you fail to do so. I haven't abandoned that book. As a matter of fact, I now have more experience that will aid me in writing it. My hope is that I will be able to do so soon. However, because of the experience of this story and the burden of my heart for sinners and fellow saints, I believe the Lord gave me this book and told me to write it first.

Anyway, back to my story. I went outside, came around to my friend's apartment window, and used the knife that I brought with me to open it. As I entered into her apartment, I started to shiver and get really nervous, but I kept going. I went into her bedroom, woke her up, and told her, "I won't hurt you." It was too late; she was already frightened, scared, hurt, and crying! Nonetheless, I proceeded in restraining and blindfolding her. I tried to disguise my voice, but she had recognized my voice, so she fought back. I was terrified! I didn't know if I should run or if I should stay and fight. There was nothing good in me being there, and there was no reason to be fighting to maximize sin and hurt.

She was crying, and I was frightened and confused! The moment I walked into her bedroom I was frightened and scared, but I didn't have the backbone to turn back. I figured I'd gone too far already; I might as well follow through. One thing I know for sure is that even though God did not override my free will by putting an impossible obstacle in my way so that I could not go through with my plan, He was still merciful and gracious enough to make me feel totally nervous, scared, and confused in what I had planned so that it would not fully materialize.

As you're reading my story, I'm sure you've already come to a correct conclusion as to what my plans were. It took me close to a year to come out of self-denial and to shamefully admit that my plans were indeed to rape her. The "R word" was too painful to say! In today's world, it seems to be even worse than a murder. But it was the truth. I could have said "nonconsensual sex" or something else, but that would be only an attempt to "pretty up" and lessen the shamefulness of something that is most disgusting!

I thought that it was best for me to give in to the short scuffle, turn the lights on, and run out of her apartment door. So I did, leaving the knife I used to open the window, the dress tie, and the tape. I quietly made my way back upstairs to my apartment while trying to eliminate the sound of my footsteps. My heart was beating faster than I could count! I had just hit the bottom of rock bottom—but there was more mess at the bottom.

FACING MY MESS

I sat there in my living room wondering, *What should I do now?* I thought of going back down to her apartment to show myself, let her know it was me, and say how truly sorry I was for doing that to her! I thought of waking my wife, who was sleeping all that time. I didn't know what to do. At the same time, I knew she would be calling the police and her parents. Before long, I looked outside and saw my own worst nightmare—the cops had arrived!

Instantly, the self-preservation of the human spirit kicked in. I started thinking of different lies I could tell. *How am I going to cover up what I just did and escape?* I wondered. The lie option that I chose for "back up" was to say that I was just playing, that it was just a stunt to scare her. It was as lame as a dead duck because deep inside I knew it was not true, and it was only a matter of time before the "duck" started to stink in me! Even if everybody believed me, my heart would not believe me. The first lie option I chose was to fabricate an outside intruder.

I couldn't sleep! I spent most of that time beating up on myself, and rightly so. Early the next morning, I decided to go outside, get some mud on my shoes, walk down to her apartment, and then walk all the way into my living room. Then I called the police and reported that someone had broken into my house. By doing this, I was hoping to direct their attention to an outside intruder. Those are the kind of lies people tell when they hit the bottom of rock bottom—unbelievable!

I even tried to convince my wife and our neighbor across from us that it had to be an outside intruder. It felt so uncomfortable because I saw the fretful look on my wife's face! She felt unsafe like anybody would, but her husband was the source of it all.

Later in the afternoon I went to pick up my wife and daughter and made a stop at the grocery store. When we got back home, the police were there again, but this time with their investigation unit. I kept going as if everything was normal, bringing up the groceries from the car. As soon as I got upstairs, one of the officers asked me if I was Raymond Moore. I said yes, and he said he couldn't let me go into my apartment. I would have to go with him for questioning.

My wife started crying, and there I was, pretending as if I was oblivious to what was going on or what the officer was saying. My wife quickly asked the neighbor if she could take our daughter so she wouldn't see the police taking her father away. Also, the officer was kind enough to ask me to come outside with him, away from everybody; when we got outside, he placed the handcuffs on me.

Never did I imagine a day like that—in the back of a police car heading for the station. After we got to the station, I was brought into a room for questioning. I decided I was going to stick to my first story, that it must have been an outside intruder who also broke into my apartment.

The officer was not convinced by my story. After talking with me for a while, he got up, went away, and came back with some evidence—the knife, tie, tape, and a Bible. I was cornered, not necessarily by the evidence, but by the Bible. When I saw the

Bible, it was as if God had walked into the room. So I broke down and confessed that it had been me; I was guilty!

However, I still kept back the full truth because I was still in denial. I reverted to the other lie option, "I was just scaring her." Looking back, I think to myself, *Who was going to buy that story? Why would anyone go through so much, even breaking the law, in order to scare a friend?* Nonetheless, I still tried to sell it.

A Cold Jail Cell

In bitter tears and anguish, I found myself in a cold jail cell! It felt like this was the end of my life, and I thought I would never see freedom again! Later that day the same officer came back to see me. I asked him if it were possible to write a letter of apology to the victim, and he said "sure." So I did, only to find out later that he didn't give it to her and that the letter was being used against me in court. I was angry! I had already confessed to everything, and there was nothing new in the letter. But what could I do? Nothing!

In court that afternoon, I told the judge that I had sinned against God and was guilty of the charges. But he was quick to stop me because I was making a guilty plea without understanding the process of the legal system and the ramifications of making a guilty plea the way I did. I had surrendered to the fact that I had sinned against the Lord. If I had to die in prison as a repentant and truly remorseful saint who had sinned, rather than as a free or incarcerated sinner who was in denial and unrepentant, that's what I was about to do.

I was quickly assigned a lawyer, and my next court date was set for a few days. This meant I would be transported to the correction center and be remanded because I was also denied bail.

The next day I was off with a group of other guys on a 45-minute drive to the corrections center.

When we arrived at the prison, I found myself among some guys who were so comfortable, as if they were in their second home; some of them had been in and out so many times they'd lost count. I was nervous, however, and felt like I was going to pee my pants—literally! As a small guy, less than 150 pounds, compared to some big, well-built guys, I felt intimidated to say the least!

In spite of it all, I felt the hand of God with me; He was going to take me through this fire and raise me up from beneath rock bottom, if for nothing else, to declare His goodness and His grace—along with His righteous justice.

Without asking me a question, the guys could tell it was my first time in jail. They could see it all over me—in my face, my speech; they just knew. In His omniscient protection, wisdom, and grace, the Lord strengthened me so as not to completely break down in tears before the other inmates because then they would have sought to take advantage of me. But as soon as I was in my cell, I could not restrain my tears! They were like a dam that had broken through its walls.

At one point I remember praying, "Lord, I cannot pay the price to wash away or even to cover my sins. Is not my life and blood the only payment that would be reasonable or at least close to it? Yet, not even my blood would be pure enough to be accepted. Will You take my life so Your justice can be satisfied? Remember, O Lord, that You paid for my sins when You carried the cross with my sins to Calvary, died, and rose again. Lord, I pray, please have mercy on me and forgive me of all my sins. All I can do is confess my sins and repent of my ungodly ways. I cannot go back and change my yesterday. Lord, in Your holy and righteous justice You have punished me. But now, O Lord, I pray that You would show me Your great love and grace twice as much!"

I was hurting so deeply that my muscles started to tighten up, and I started having chest pains! I could not sleep either. I thought I was about to have a heart attack and had to go and see the nurse, who wanted to load me up with medications. But I didn't take them. I was always weak and had continuous headaches. I was hungry, while still feeling like I was full. I could understand some of the feelings that David wrote about when, for example he said, *"My heart is stricken and withered like grass, so that I forget to eat my bread"* (Ps. 102:4). I had some of the weirdest and most severe feelings in my body, feelings that I didn't even know existed—some of which I don't even know how to describe!

THE COURT DECISION

While I was trying to deal with me, my family was trying to arrange my case and get a lawyer. So I went to court again, but this time I had my case postponed because the lawyer issue wasn't finalized yet. Eventually I got a lawyer and ended up talking with him on the phone from the remand unit. He informed me of the seriousness of my crimes and that the sentence range for some of these crimes went all the way up to life in prison—namely breaking and entering or unlawful entry of a residence. When he told me that, it felt like my heart had stopped beating! I was breathless; he had to ask me if I was still on the other line.

The details were ironed out, and I was on my way to court again. This time though, I was going to learn my fate. My lawyer let me know that he had been talking with the prosecutor and was working on a plea bargain. I was all for it because I was not about to let my family waste a lot of money taking my case to trial when I knew in fact that I was guilty. So I went to court with my hopes up (maybe unrealistically) that I would be given a sentence of house arrest with community service and probation.

I had a long letter that I was going to read to the judge and also to the family of the victim, whom I assumed would be there. The judge didn't let me read it because it was too long. Instead I shared from the depths of my heart, crying and trembling, how sorry I was, saying that I took full responsibility for my actions and that I was asking for mercy in the midst of justice!

The prosecutor was merciless, and things weren't looking good for me. He gave me a picture of what it might be like in Heaven as the accuser of the brethren (satan) accuses the saints before God day and night (see Rev. 12:10). If we only sin an "inch," he's going to take a magnifying glass and make it into a foot, while bringing up every negative thing of the past! No wonder we need grace and truth—the blood of the Lamb and the word of our testimony (see Rev. 12:11).

Eventually the judge, after hearing and examining the records of my life, spoke out and said, "How can someone who is making his way up the ladder of life and has so much going on for him, do something like this?"

Then my lawyer, Mr. Parker, a Christian man who had known me indirectly over the years, said, "Your honor, King David, a man after God's own heart, committed adultery, and when he found out that the woman was pregnant, he had her husband killed." At that point the judge replied, "That's the story with…ahh…Bathsheba? And my lawyer said, "Yes, sir."

The prosecutor and my lawyer went back and forth as to what my sentence should be while I was fighting to keep my knees from knocking together. Soon after, the judge adjourned the case till after lunch for sentencing. To make a long story short, after lunch my sentence was handed down—14 months with time served, along with three years of probation. Though I was hoping for a sentence of house arrest (maybe unrealistically), it didn't happen. It was devastating! At the same time, it could have been much worse. They took me out of the court room and brought me to the station in preparation to transfer me to the correction center.

OVERWHELMED BY GRIEF

Shortly afterward, my family came to the station to see me before I was sent off. I never imagined the possibility of being in jail. Having my parents see me there, guilty of that particular crime, was gut-wrenching. I was in deep tears! My wife, parents, brother, and mother-in-law were all trying to be strong for me because I was weak. My dad said to me, "You got to be strong and stay strong. Don't cry!" While my mom on the other hand said, "Don't tell him not to cry. Cry, son; let it out!"

It was hard! I understood where both of them were coming from. My dad didn't want me to become so weak and depressed that I would be tempted just to give up. He wanted me to squeeze it back in and put on a strong face. And my mom didn't want me to allow all the feelings of remorse, hurt, pain, and guilt to stay inside and overwhelm me; she wanted me to cry and pour it all out!

If I were to muster up all the power within me, I could not have stopped myself from crying! My tears overpowered me. This was not just sorrow or remorse over the fact that I was caught; it was deeper than that—it was godly sorrow that was about to lead me into true repentance. I had sinned against God and brought reproach to His name and His people—giving the enemy grounds to profane the name of the Lord and Christians. I felt like I was a big disappointment to God, and indeed I was.

I wasn't having a pity party about me and over me. My tears were also of sincere concern for the victim of my most despicable actions. Would she be able to sleep at night? Was she having reoccurring nightmares? How will she react when she hears a little noise in or outside of her apartment? How will she deal with a possible future relationship with her husband? Is she going to be terrified every time her husband touches her because of flashbacks? Will she be fearful and skeptical of having male friends? These were some of the thoughts that fueled my tears.

I thought about my family, also. What if someone had done to my wife, daughter, sister, or mother what I had just done; how would I take it? How would I feel? I'm sure I would be feeling the utmost outrage! I failed to look beyond my actions to see the far-reaching implications. But that's how sin often limits the eyes of our mind to see only the satisfaction of the moment and not the "and then what?" consequences.

Jesus said in Matthew 7:12, "*Therefore, whatever you want men to do to you, do also to them, for this is the Law and the Prophets.*" Though I did not sexually assault her, it didn't take away from the fact that the court saw right through to my intentions—my heart was even guiltier than my actions.

I also thought about how this would affect my future relationship with my wife. So many different thoughts were going through my mind. I didn't know if she would still love me and forgive me. Even though she assured me of her support, a part of me still wondered if she was planning to call our marriage quits, but didn't want to make things any harder for me while I was in jail. Was she just waiting till I got out to let it all out? She has been more than a helpmate to me! Through everything, she stood by me, knowing very well how others might view me; because she chose to stand beside me, others might also view her negatively. When it was easy to leave, she took the hard way and stayed. She was truly hurt, and I know it was her love for me and the grace of God that kept us together! I bless God for her then as much as I do today!

How Do I Pray?

So there I was in prison and wondering if I would be assaulted by some huge, well-built, 200-plus-pound gay inmate. It was a scary thought! But the hand of the Lord was with me, and He gave me favor with the inmates, most of the guards, and the chaplain.

At first, however, I had tremendous inner struggles! I couldn't pray because my emotions were silencing my words. I couldn't pray according to my integrity—that too was shattered and wasn't all that genuine to begin with. Neither could I pray from a self-esteem point of view—there was no good opinion about me. Even though I'd done some good things in the past— what I had just done had overshadowed *everything!* It was very easy to utterly hate myself. But I could not hate myself, even though I had to hate my sinful and outrageous behavior!

Since praying was a challenge, I resorted to writing out my feelings. This song was penned shortly after I got to the prison, when I was dealing with these specific struggles:

How Do I Pray...?

Vs. 1) I'm on a journey going to my promised land. It's where God wants me, and it's where I want to be. But along the way I stumbled and fell in sin—condemnation comes, it tries to keep me from rising again.

Chr.) How do I pray when my integrity does not defend me? How do I pray when I've made a mess of my life—when all I see is the darkness surrounding me? I've got to pray and take God at His word. A broken heart and contrite spirit God will not turn away.

Vs. 2) Lord I need You; I cannot make it on my own. Please stand by me; show Your awesome power again because You care, and Your love won't leave me here. Yes I'm delayed, but I know I'm not denied.

Vs. 3) I know God loves me, but it hurts Him when I fall. I may have to wander, and it may take a little bit longer. I know You'll be there to answer when I call; even though I'm not sure just what to say.

Brg.) If I call from the depths of my heart, I know You will answer. When my words can't be heard I know You'll read my tears.

Though it felt like I was in hell, the Spirit of God brought me back to the truth of His unchanging Word, regardless of my feelings and situation. That's when, and only when, I was truly able to pray—although I still had days of ups and downs.

I also found courage in the fact that if King David and Moses were alive today, they would be in prison with me. Maybe this wasn't the greatest way to find consolation, but it helped. Consolation didn't come from David, who sinned and was forgiven, but rather from God who forgave him. David was just an object lesson, so to speak; I got the lesson—the principle. Certainly, it is never a good way to go about finding consolation—by looking at what others have done or haven't done in comparison to yourself. But it is also an undeniable fact that the Scriptures include the sins of the saints and those who were lifestyle sinners to give hope to all who are willing to put their trust in a merciful and forgiving God.

POWER OF TESTIMONY

It was this fact, many years ago, that encouraged my faith in God for healing. When I was 13 years old and trusted in God to heal me of my heart disease, my faith in God's healing power was based on knowledge—the historical acts of God as recorded in the Bible. I concluded, if God could part the Red Sea (see Exod. 14), then the sickness was nothing for Him.

If He could deliver Daniel from the lions' den (see Dan. 6) and the three Hebrew boys from the fiery furnace (see Dan. 3); if He could raise Lazarus from the dead (see John 11), if He could calm the raging storm with just a word from His mouth (see Matt. 8:23-27); if He could provide water in the wilderness (see Exod. 17:1-7); if He could touch Sarah's dead womb and bring it back to life (see Gen. 21:1-8); surely He was able to heal me. These were the stories they taught in Sunday school and children's church. I exercised my faith in God based on these truths, and God healed me. No longer did I have to keep taking those injections.

Just as these great stories of miraculous power and God being faithful to His faithful saints helped me at a crucial juncture in my life, I was also encouraged in prison by the stories of God remaining faithful to His unfaithful saints when they cried out to Him in repentance. If we teach that David was a faithful saint, but one who sinned and whom God forgave, we're not implying that people can do whatever they want because God will forgive them. Instead, we'll be preaching the whole story, or at least the other, not-so-familiar side of it. It will certainly be of help, if and when people fall and find themselves down in the valley along their journey. The fact is that saints do sin and sinners become saints. God's pardoning grace is available to both.

I reasoned with the Scriptures and came up with the conclusion that Joseph was in prison because of his steadfast integrity, and God remained faithful to His promise—He was with Joseph and brought him to his destiny (see Gen 37; 39-50). And I was in prison because of a lack of integrity. So did that mean God could not and would not bring me to the destiny He had planned for me? I concluded, no.

I said, "O that God would use me, a 21st-century "Joseph," who is as guilty as can be, to show the other side of His all-surpassing power and loving grace and mercy, to give assurance of His redeeming grace to the saints who sin and the sinners who are living in sin and are seeking a way out."

Nobody brought this situation on me; I brought it on myself. In other words, like the psalmist David said, *"If I make my bed in hell…"* (Ps. 139:8). I had definitely made my bed in hell—the pit—the bottom of rock bottom! But I came to the understanding that even if I make my bed in hell, then even there, God is with me. And He's not just there to watch me burn in my shame and sorrow; He's there to pull me up, rescue me, and lead me in the paths of righteousness for His name's sake. The darkness cannot conquer me because the Light of the world is in me and with me. I owe Him my all, and I give Him all the glory!

In Second Chronicles 7:14 God says,

If My people who are called by My name will humble them-selves, and pray and seek My face, and turn from their wicked ways, then will I hear from heaven, and forgive their sin and heal their land.

I was going to hold on to that promise with everything that was in me.

MANY TEARS

"I need You now more than ever," I said in prayer. "If You don't save me, then I will lose my mind—my heart is about to give up! I'm trying to be strong, but I've just about tried enough! My strength is gone! My hope and my faith are just barely hanging on. Do You not see my pain? Do You not see what I'm going through? Do You not care? If You don't answer me, jail will be the last place...!

"Does a father hear his child crying out for help and not help? Aren't You my Abba Father? Am I not crying loud enough for You to hear me? Am I not hurting enough yet? Is my punishment too light? Am I not repentant enough? Can I possibly be more repentant and remorseful over my sins than I already am? If so, maybe I just don't know how. I have given You my all! What more can I give? I am only human, Your creation—flesh and bones, made out of the dust of the earth.

If You don't understand me or if my words are not really making any sense, then I graciously ask You to please search my heart, study my heart. Analyze my heart and attend to it! It needs You! It's crying out to You!"

This prayer, by the way, is a word-for-word prayer taken from the many letters I wrote as I was journaling my experience.

Truthfully, this season of my life brought more tears to me than all other times in my entire life combined. It was definitely urgent that I get my hands on a Bible! I had to preach to myself and encourage myself in the Lord. I had to find strength in order not to self destruct.

THE BOTTOM OF THE BOTTOM

Going to prison was like hitting the bottom, but what got me there and the things I had to deal with emotionally and spiritually were the bottom of the bottom. It was as if I fell through the bottom of the rock and the weight of the rock was now on me! The weight was unbearable! I can honestly testify that if God had not sustained me, I would not have survived to tell my story.

I remember one night in particular, I had a vision. I saw in the vision two men standing on the inside of my cell door (whom I had to believe were angels). Outside I saw demonic spirits of insanity and suicide, who also looked like normal men, trying to force their way in. As they pushed to come in, the angels would brace themselves firmly to withstand the push. While this was going on for about a minute, I was literally shaking and sweating on my bed! I could feel the effect of the spiritual battle that was going on—just as you can feel the effects of a plane going through turbulence.

In my weakness and pain, the devil saw an opportunity to destroy me. He wanted me to end my life or to end up going to live in some mental institution. But God had invested too much in me, and He was going to protect His investment for the glory of His own name—yes, for His name's sake, not mine. The landing at destiny was not and is not to be in jail.

I knew the spirits were demonic spirits of insanity and suicide because the angels told me. They also told me that they had come to protect me. Though I had comfort in the fact that the angels were there, it was still a scary sight and feeling! It was a dark place to be in. That prison was filled with just about every different kind of demonic spirit with varying assignments.

This was not a figment of my imagination—a made-up story to add some drama to my experience. God is my witness to the reality of all my experiences during this season of my life, including this vision. I am telling the truth for the sake of the truth and not for anything else.

That night I felt like I was literally experiencing this Scripture: *"...when the enemy comes in like a flood, the Spirit of the LORD will lift up a standard against him"* (Isa. 59:19). Inmates were cutting themselves, committing suicide, sexually and physically assaulting each other, doing drugs—you name it, and it was going on there. It was only God who kept me from suicide, from insanity, from being assaulted—it was God! Why did He do it? I really don't know. I would like to believe He did it because I am His child, His saint who had sinned and needed His merciful hands to reach deep down to the bottom of rock bottom and rescue me—and because I was repentant.

Less Than I Deserved

Though I could see that the Lord was disciplining me, I knew I wasn't getting what I deserved. As I read Ezekiel 20:44, I felt like it was a prophetic word being declared to me personally. *"Then you shall know that I am the LORD, when I have dealt with you for My name's sake, not according to your wicked ways nor according to your corrupt doings..."* From that came this song:

You Compensate Me With Grace

Vs. 1) While You were on the cross receiving God's justice, You were pouring out God's grace to all. I was Your enemy, yet You died for me. You didn't pay me back what I deserved...

Chr.) ...Instead You compensate me with grace. You gave me what I didn't deserve. You didn't give me what I truly deserved.

Brg.) Thank You
Lord Thank You
Lord
Thank You Lord
Thank You Lord

My prayer was like that of David, *"Remember the word to Your servant, upon which You have caused me to hope. This is my comfort in my affliction, for Your word has given me life"* (Ps. 119:49-50).

In the midst of my deepest trouble and pain, the Lord led me to a book that was beat up and battered, floating around on the unit—*In the Eye of the Storm* by Max Lucado. This book is one of the most powerful books I've ever read, and it entered my life with such perfect timing. Without a doubt, I saw God's sustaining power at work, using that book to keep me alive in the midst of my storm.

I know what it's like to feel like your life is over and all hope is gone. I know what it's like not to have any crutch to lean on. I know what it's like to literally be in a dark place—alone, frightened, and hurting! I know what it's like to be in a physical prison, a shame prison, and an emotional prison all at the same time. I know what it's like not just to be at the breaking point, but to be completely broken and shattered!

I know what it's like to have no one to call to but God! Sure I could have called out to the guards, but they certainly would not have sympathized. Neither would I have wanted to jeopardize my safety with the other inmates by yelling for the guards at 3 A.M. when I couldn't sleep.

This psalm shed some light on what I was feeling and wanted to say, but didn't know how to put together:

O Lord, God of my salvation, I have cried out day and night before You. Let my prayer come before You; incline Your ear to my cry. For my soul is full of troubles, and my life draws near to the grave. I am counted with those who go down to the pit; I am like a man who has no strength, adrift among the dead, like the slain who lie in the grave, whom You remember no more, and who are cut off from Your hand. You have laid me in the lowest pit, in darkness, in the depths. Your wrath lies heavy upon me, and You have afflicted me with all Your waves. You have put my acquaintances far from me, You have made me an abomination to them; I am shut up, and I cannot get out; my eye wastes away because of affliction... (Psalm 88:1-9).

I have learned that one of the most painful aspects of suffering is the loneliness of it. Others may offer their support and sympathy, but no one can really put on your shoes and walk the journey with you and for you. Even if, for example, someone is dealing with the same kind of cancer you've had to deal with, it is very likely that they're also dealing with a combination of other issues that are different from yours. This pretty much makes every situation unique, though there may be many similarities. Our individual struggles are lonely, and only God can truly meet us in them and provide the deepest comfort that our hearts crave.

SYMPATHY FOR THE OFFENDER

A big part of my loneliness also stemmed from the isolation I felt as an offender. Everyone rightly has sympathy for the victim. As the offender, I was the bad guy, and even after I had repented, it seemed like people struggled to feel sympathetically toward me.

I've noticed that most books that deal with hurts and misfortunes, such as sexual, physical, verbal, or emotional abuse, present it to the readers from a victim's point of view. These authors share their stories of rising above the abuse of their past to be victors over their victimization. They say things like, "You may be struggling with hurts from the past or dealing with low self-esteem stemming from all the painful experiences you've endured. God sees and knows your pain, and if you're willing to turn it over to Him, He will turn things around for you. I was there, and if He can do it for me, I know He can do it for you."

This message is so important for so many people's lives, and I do not at all want to demean it. We all have experienced or will experience hurts at the hands of others. And we all need to learn to be victors, not victims. But I also want to draw attention to the needs and hurts of the offenders. Though they were in the wrong, we must care about their souls and reach out to provide hope and healing if they are willing.

We don't often think about how the offender emotionally and spiritually deals with his actions, which caused deep and irreversible hurt to a victim. Their guilt does not negate the validity of their struggle or pain; it should not remove them from our care and concern. (Offenders, in the broadest sense, aren't just those who've committed criminal activities, but any who have hurt and victimized others.) Jesus is not just out to save victims, but offenders too. The Lord said in Jeremiah 3:1,

> *"They say, 'If a man divorces his wife, and she goes from him and becomes another man's, may he return to her again?' Would not that land be greatly polluted? But you have played the harlot with many lovers; yet return to Me," says the Lord.*

Jesus asked for forgiveness for the men (the offenders) who were crucifying Him (see Luke 23:26-43). But as humans, looking from the viewpoint of a victim, our tendency is to hope for lightning to zap the offender on the spot.

Many stories have been told from the viewpoint of victims, but very few have been told from an offender's or convict's point of view. If offenders are not emotionless, cold-blooded criminals at heart (though some of them are), then it's more than likely that they have struggles and hurts to deal with too—though they may be different in context and are almost all self-inflicted.

While victims or others might be struggling with forgiving offenders, offenders are struggling with forgiving themselves. While victims are dealing with the hurt that was done to them, offenders are dealing with the hurt they caused—and so on.

Victims need help and hope, and so do offenders. I believe this is the understanding behind the justice system's endeavor to have different programs to facilitate the rehabilitation of convicts of various crimes.

Offenders still have their own issues and consequences to deal with, stemming from their own actions. And that's where people tend to be unsympathetic—though that is certainly understandable. I personally had a brother who was killed over 20 years ago, and I can still remember the feelings that I had toward the guy who killed him. They weren't nice at all, and as a little boy I wanted to take things into my own hands and get revenge. So in a sense I can have true sympathy even though I am an offender. (It might be disadvantageous at times to try and reach out to both victims and offenders. The professionals would not recommend it, but would have different parties attend to different sides to avoid a conflict of interests.)

Prison ministries don't go into prisons telling convicts, "Great job; keep it up." No, God forbid! They go in with Christ, in the hope of making these bad men and women good men and women who will have something positive to offer their families and communities. These men and women whom society would like to keep at arm's length will, for the most part, be reintroduced into society; therefore, they are worth the effort.

At the same time, while I have deep concern for offenders, I am, of course, an advocate for victims, many of whom are women! Women should not be subject to the will of men, whether for pleasure or for convenience. Some of us men think that women should be at our disposal—cooking, cleaning, grocery shopping, doing laundry, and so forth. It's about time men start treating women with the love and care they deserve! They are not of less value. They are not our subordinates. It grieves me how many women have become victims of various types of abuse, and it grieves me that I too have victimized a woman.

DAVID AND BATHSHEBA

Reading about the sinful events surrounding the story of David and Bathsheba, it would almost seem as if David was the victim, especially when he was mourning, fasting, and praying to God for his sick child who eventually died (see 2 Sam. 12:15-23). But he was certainly not the victim. The true victim in this story was Bathsheba. She was summoned to satisfy the king's desire. Her husband was killed as a result of the king's desire and request. And on top of all that, she was carrying the king's baby while mourning the death of her husband. Then shortly after her baby was born, she had to mourn the death of her baby too.

Yes, perhaps she had a part to play in the whole thing; perhaps she didn't resist at all—but maybe she did. Just because people don't show their outward physical disapproval and resistance to something or someone, doesn't mean they're approving of whatever they're doing and welcome it. It's possible that because of some form of fear, they go along with it, yet deep in their hearts they're as regretful and resistant as possible! Either way, whether she fully resisted or not, initially she suffered way more than David did.

The Bible doesn't focus much on Bathsheba because David was the highlight of the story. But I'm sure Bathsheba has her version of the story, one that would show her as a victim of the king—David.

I am no more a victim than David was. The victim in my story is my Christian sister who suffered tremendous hurt as a result of my behavior and whose plight isn't mentioned nearly enough in my story. This was not done completely inadvertently, but simply because only she can do her story justice, as was briefly done by her victim impact statement. And as the offender, only I can do my story justice because no one can truly describe what I went through. I myself find it challenging and way too shameful.

If I'm a victim in any way, I would be a victim of my own hypocrisy and of abandonment from the Church community. But in the context of my crime itself, I wouldn't dare equate myself with the true victim! I know the pain, at least partially, of a victim because I created one and heard the hurt, fear, trauma, insecurity, discomfort, and so forth that was read out in the courtroom from her victim impact statement.

In Defense of Women

God does not force us to do His good and righteous will. Much less should any of us force others to do our sinful will. Many are living in abusive relationships and don't know how to get out. Some, on the other hand, are forced into all sorts of relationships and dress codes, especially in many Middle Eastern countries. Women should have as many rights as men do. How come, for instance, we never hear of a man being stoned to death or punished for adultery in some of these strict Islamic countries? Is it only the women who commit adultery? My appeal to men, Christian and non-Christian alike, is that we would treat women the way we would like other men to treat our daughters. (By the way, it's not only men who exploit children and women in general; women also exploit children and other women.)

As I sit and write this book, I have a loving wife, two daughters, and a son. It would so hurt my heart if someone did to any of my children or wife what I did to my victim. As men, we wouldn't like to see our five-year-old abducted for who knows what, so we shouldn't do it to another. We wouldn't like to hear that our 15-year-old or wife was assaulted, harassed, or stalked, so we shouldn't do it to another. And if we are in the position to stop someone else from doing it, we must do it for the sake of another. For every time it happens, there is a victim, and the violation hurts and leaves irreversible scars!

I understand that might be a little hard to swallow, considering who it's coming from. I have learned a great deal about how awful the affects of abuse can be—though I desperately wish I had learned it a different way. That is part of why I have shared my story—in hopes that others may learn from my sins and choose not to create more victims.

God has shown and taught me so much during this time in my life, and for the good He has brought to me out of my bad, I am truly thankful! As despicable as my story is, I hope you can gain some benefit from it. I feel like I've just laid down my heart on the ground, knowing very well it may be trampled on.

ENDNOTE

1. See http://www.christianpost.com/article/20070605/porn-addiction-flooding-culture-church/.

CHAPTER 7

ABRAHAM'S STORY

The Lie Behind the Hidden Truth

 Let nothing be done through selfish ambition or conceit, but in lowliness of mind let each esteem others better than himself. Let each of you look out not only for his own interest, but also for the interests of others (Philippians 2:3-4).

There wasn't anything special about me, Abraham, as far as I know, and I don't know why the Lord chose me rather than another. I wasn't more righteous than the other members of my family or my neighbors. The Lord chose me out of His sovereign power and election. He called and commissioned me to a purpose that would ultimately be a blessing to the entire world. My goal was to succeed in all that I was called to be and do. Therefore, abandoning my purpose or dying before its fulfillment was not an option.

This driving force, however, led me to become a selfish, inconsiderate liar! My belief was that I had to protect myself at any cost with regard to the promise, even if it meant lying about my relationship with my wife, which resulted in another man taking her from me—not just once, but twice.

This was the initial call of the Lord on my life as stated in the Book of Genesis:

Now the LORD had said to Abram: "Get out of your country, from your family and from your father's house, to a land that I will show you. I will make you a great nation; I will bless you and make your name great; and you shall be a blessing. I will bless those who bless you, and I will curse him who curses you; and in you all the families of the earth shall be blessed" (Genesis 12:1-3).

I did not fully obey what the Lord had commanded me. There wasn't much of a problem leaving my country or my people, but leaving my father's house brought up some issues. When my wife and I decided to begin our journey to this new land, my father, being the head of the family, decided he, along with my nephew Lot, should come with us. The Lord's plan was for Sarah and me to go to the land of Canaan alone, but my father decided he had to come. And on top of that, he then decided we should dwell in the land of Haran (see Gen. 11:26; 12:1-4). It was a mistake!

We must not hold on to what God wants us to let go of, and we shouldn't allow it to hold on to us either. That's the dilemma I found myself in, and it wasn't a good experience. It took the death of my father to bring me back on track in God's will. But even after the death of my father, I still took Lot along with me to Canaan. That was another eye-opener.

Shortly after my father died, I started off on the journey to the land of Canaan with Lot, Sarah, my servants, and much livestock that I had accumulated. When we got to Canaan, the Lord appeared to me again and reaffirmed His promise that to me and my descendants He would give this land (see Gen. 13:14-17). It was a big promise. The only problem with it, however, was that my wife was barren.

THE HALF TRUTH

There was a severe famine in the land, so we journeyed further south into the land of Egypt. All I could think about was God's plan for my life. It permeated my every thought, so much so that I became very inconsiderate and thought of ways to look out for and protect my own interests. I feared for my life because of Sarah. She was very beautiful, and I thought the Egyptians would kill me and take her. So I told her that whenever we journeyed to a new region where my life might be in danger because of her, I would say, "She's my sister," and she should say, "He's my brother."

In all honesty, Sarah was indeed my sister. She was the daughter of my father, but not of the same mother—she was my half sister. (In our day, such unions were allowed.) When I would say, "She's my sister," technically I was being truthful. There was also, still, a hidden truth and a lie that would paint a different picture, but I withheld it. It is this hidden truth I would like to uncover and the mindset that caused me to lie about it.

Here is how the Bible records the two events when I said Sarah was my sister. (My name had not yet been changed from Abram to Abraham or Sarah's from Sarai in the first incident.)

This is the first event:

So it was, when Abram came into Egypt, that the Egyptians saw the woman, that she was very beautiful. The princes of Pharaoh also saw her and commended her to Pharaoh. And the woman was taken to Pharaoh's house. He treated Abram well for her sake. He had sheep, oxen, male donkeys, male and female servants, female donkeys, and camels. But the LORD plagued Pharaoh and his house with great plagues because of Sarai, Abram's wife. And Pharaoh called Abram and said, "What is this you have done to me? Why did you not tell me that she was your wife? Why did you say, 'She is my sister'? I might have taken her as my wife. Now therefore, here is your wife; take her and go your way." So Pharaoh commanded his men concerning him; and they sent him away, with his wife and all that he had (Genesis 12:14-20).

Here's the second event:

And Abraham journeyed from there to the South, and dwelt between Kadesh and Shur, and stayed in Gerar. Now Abraham said of Sarah his wife, "She is my sister." And Abimelech king of Gerar sent and took Sarah. But God came to Abimelech in a dream by night, and said to him, "Indeed you are a dead man because of the woman whom you have taken, for she is a man's wife." But Abimelech had not come near her; and he said, "Lord, will You slay a righteous nation also? Did he not say to me, 'She is my sister'? And she, even herself said, 'He is my brother.' In the integrity of my heart and the innocence of my hands I have done this." And God said to him in a dream, "Yes, I know that you did this in the integrity of your heart. For I also withheld you from sinning against Me; therefore I did not let you touch her. Now therefore, restore the man's wife; for he is a prophet, and he will pray for you and you shall live. But if you do not restore her, know that you shall surely die, you and all who are yours." So Abimelech rose early in the morning, called all his servants, and told all these things in their hearing; and the men were very much afraid.

And Abimelech called Abraham and said to him, "What have you done to us? How have I offended you, that you have brought on me and on my kingdom a great sin? You have done deeds to me that ought not to be done." Then Abimelech said to Abraham, "What did you have in view, that you have done this thing?" And Abraham said, "Because I thought, surely the fear of God is not in this place; and they will kill me on account of my wife. But indeed she is truly my sister. She is the daughter of my father, but not the daughter of my mother; and she became my wife" (Genesis 20:1-12).

I was selfish and inconsiderate where my wife was concerned. Her safety was never really a priority; it was all about my safety, my goodwill, and my survival. Did I give thought to the fact that she could become someone else's wife or concubine or that, because of her beauty, she could become an entertainment girl for the king and his officials?

For goodness sake, she could have been abused by some stranger, raped, and killed! I must admit that I gave thought to all those scenarios, but unfortunately they weren't enough to deter me from doing what I did. I certainly did not exercise true love. I didn't give myself for her; I gave her up for me.

I'm not sure if Sarah was 100 percent behind my survival plan, knowing that she would likely be putting herself in the arms of the unknown. Nonetheless, she went along with the decision because she really loved me, respected my decisions, and was very submissive (not forcibly or in a negative way). Later on, I wondered if her strong love for me had blinded her to my selfishness.

The agreement was more than what I had bargained for. Night after night I went to bed all alone and cold. There was no one to cuddle with during those long, cold nights, no one to share my day and life with. My wife was in the palace, possibly in the arms of another man. I missed my wife dearly and wondered how she was doing! I pondered on how to get us out of this mess, but none of my scenarios was feasible. Then, there was the thought of journeying to another city, but I could not and would not, because Sarah was in the king's palace—the prison of lust. Had God not intervened, I'm not sure how it would have all turned out.

THE HIDDEN TRUTH

Sarah was indeed my sister, but she was also my wife. However, whenever I thought my life, and not hers, was in danger, I would say, "She is my sister," and she was supposed to say, "He's my brother." Personally, I would not consider myself innocent or a credible witness. I know I lied—not by declaring something true when it was false or vice versa, but by not declaring the truth in its entirety. I was very deliberate in saying she is my sister when I knew for a fact the question asked was mainly pertaining to the other side of the truth that was unspoken, or hidden.

I declared part of the truth, while consciously refusing to declare the rest. It would have been different if my wife wasn't so beautiful and my life wasn't in danger because of her. If that were the case, and I were to allege that she was just my sister, I would have no need to feel guilty—my heart would not have condemned me for withholding information that I didn't know was required of me.

On the contrary, if and when my life wasn't in danger, I had no problem professing that she was my wife. As a matter of fact, I was boastful about my wife's inner and external beauty! Nonetheless, the lie behind the hidden truth was not in what I said or even in what I didn't say; it was in the motive of my heart that silenced the voice. Unlike Rahab's lie, which was motivated by faith and trust in God (see Josh. 2), mine was driven by selfishness, fear, and a lack of trust in the Almighty.

It is possible to speak the truth with manipulative and destructive motives. In such cases, the truth remains the truth, but the motive is not—it's a lie. This is called doing the right thing with the wrong motive and for the wrong reason.

DOING IT MY OWN WAY

Maybe a part of why I did what I did was because God had not yet revealed to me that it was through Sarah that He would give me a child and birth a great nation—not to mention the fact that she was barren. God had made the promise to me, but not necessarily to Sarah. So as far as I was concerned, He could have given me another wife. I was also concerned that they would kill me and take my wife because the *"fear of the Lord was not in this place"* (Gen. 20:11). My excuse was a crutch. Even if that were the case, it showed that I didn't trust God enough to believe He could preserve us through anything. Selfish and inconsiderate people will always find reasons to justify their actions—even twisting God's Word for their own benefit.

Eventually the Lord made it clear that He would fulfill His promise through Sarah and that she would be the mother of many nations (see Gen. 17:15-16). Prior to its fulfillment, I tried to abandon the promise of being a biological father because of all the impossible realities we were facing by asking the Lord to accept the son of Eliezer, my servant, as the son of promise. The Lord said, "No" (see Gen. 15:1-5).

Sarah, also, got impatient and frustrated with the unfulfilled promise and decided to give me her maid, Hagar, to be my wife so we could have children by her—like a surrogate mother. So Hagar became my wife and very shortly after became pregnant. Now, with it being evident to all that she was pregnant, she began to despise Sarah to the point of bragging in her face in subtle and blatant ways. Then, when Sarah couldn't take it anymore, she began blaming me. But to be honest, I was becoming more attached to Hagar because she was carrying my child. It was turning into a messy family affair (see Gen. 16).

THE MESSY AFFAIR

When the situation became overwhelming for Sarah, and after she kept blaming me for the present predicament, I told her to do with Hagar whatever seemed best to her. After all, Hagar was her maid. So she began treating Hagar harshly until the maid couldn't take it anymore and ran away. But the Angel of the Lord met her in the wilderness and spoke to her, telling her to go back to her mistress and making her a promise concerning her unborn baby. So she came back home (see Gen. 16:7-12).

I could have saved myself a lot of trouble if I had waited on the Lord and hadn't had anything to do with Hagar. Believe me, though; it was not easy waiting on the Lord for so long. God forbid that I should pretend like I was some super saint who never got impatient or frustrated and never questioned God in regard to this awesome promise and plan. My faith in God's ability was unwavering, but I can't really say I had unwavering confidence in myself, my ability. Even though God had initiated and entered into this covenant with me through the shedding of blood and bound Himself to it, I still questioned the possibility of the timing because time was running out for me and Sarah.

We learned our lesson the hard way. Going ahead of God and trying to help Him in our own understanding is never a wise thing to do. There would not have been an Ishmael if we had waited on God.

Not long after Hagar returned, Ishmael was born. Things were going from bad to worse, so much so that I could see it leading to a fist fight. Sarah kept nagging me about the mess that "we" had created when it was her idea and decision to begin with.

PROMISE FULFILLED

During that time, the Lord kept reassuring me of His promise through various means—changing our names, the sign of circumcision, visitation, vision, and encouragement (see Gen. 15; 17; 18). When the Lord told me I would have a son by Sarah—who overheard and laughed in her heart because, not only was she still barren, but she was also now 90 years old and I was 100—I was again strengthened in my faith (see Gen. 17:17-18).

The Lord declared to us that, regardless of the impossibilities that we were facing and the confusion and skepticism of our hearts, we would have a son and should call his name Isaac. Then the Lord said to me,

> *Why did Sarah laugh, saying, "Shall I surely bear a child, since I am old?" Is there anything too hard for the LORD? At the appointed time I will return to you, according to the time of life, and Sarah shall have a son* (Genesis 18:13-14).

So it was declared, and so it happened. Sarah became pregnant and gave birth to the son of promise, Isaac (see Gen. 21:1-8).

Nothing brought more joy to Sarah and me than the birth of Isaac! He wasn't just a son born to a barren woman (and to seniors), but he was the son of promise. However, this celebration was often overshadowed by strife between Sarah and Hagar. After Isaac was born, things went from bad to worse. To make a long story short, Hagar and Ishmael were sent away so we could devote our life and resources to our son of promise (see Gen. 21:9-21).

PRAYING FOR LOT

Just before Isaac was born, there arose a situation that brought about the eye-opener that I mentioned earlier. A few years before, Lot and I had to separate because our livestock were too many for us to dwell together, and contention was rising between our herdsmen. So I gave Lot the first pick of what part of the land he would choose; he chose the best part (see Gen. 13:5-12).

I allowed Lot to choose first because, even though I knew he would choose the best part, God had promised me the entire land. I knew what God had promised and called me to, so I was not terrified or intimidated by someone else going ahead of me. I could watch Lot take the better portion, even though he did not earn or deserve it, knowing that God had decreed it for me. I was in God's will, and I knew He would fight my battles.

Little did Lot or I know that the place he chose, with all the fertile plains as far as Sodom, would become a place permeated with homosexuality and perversion. God told me His plan to destroy Sodom and Gomorrah, and I pleaded with the Lord not to destroy it. Physically, I had intervened on Lot's behalf in the past when he was taken captive by invading kings (see Gen. 14:13-16), but now I was interceding spiritually on his behalf.

CONSEQUENCES FOR GENERATIONS

I could share a lot more about my relationship with my son Isaac, especially about when the Lord tested me to sacrifice my son on Mount Moriah. But the primary point of my story here is the fact that, even though I was the father of faith, I had issues like every other person.

The lies that I told became a trend that was passed on to my children. Isaac told an identical lie, except that his wife Rebekah was his cousin (see Gen. 26:1-11; 24:1-67). Then Isaac's son, Jacob, deceived him in order to steal his brother's birthright blessing after he had already deceptively gained his brother's birthright (see Gen. 25:27-34; 27:1-41). Then, Jacob's sons, 12 in all, sold their brother, Joseph, and lied to their father to make it seem as if, *"wild beast had devoured him"* (see Gen. 37:18-35). This was the evil generational pattern I set in motion—troubling to say the least.

My name and fame is not free of tarnish and shame—earthly shame that is. It might not be as significant as some of the others, but it doesn't matter. I needed mercy, forgiveness, and grace like everyone else.

RAY'S REFLECTIONS AND INSIGHTS

The first thing that stands out to me about Abraham's story is that the plan and purpose that God calls us to requires that we give something up. We have to let go of something or maybe someone. Jesus didn't come to call sinners, but to call sinners to repentance—they must turn from sin and the things that are weighing them down so they can run their race and run to Him. In other words, let go and let God.

To follow after God requires self-denial. For example, Olympians don't live like ordinary people, so to speak. Their diets are unique, and so is their discipline. As the Olympics draw nearer, the rigidness of their discipline and practice intensifies. All of their hard work, training, and self-denial are not done with the hope of just making it to the Olympics and being called an Olympian. They are done with a deep desire to be a champion Olympian.

For Abraham, it was as if he was on his way to the Olympics (God's promise), but wasn't strong and committed enough to change anything and incorporate any disciplines into his life. He was bringing all the weight and baggage along. His father and nephew should not have been with him. He was commanded to let them go, and his lack of obedience caused him to spend years waiting in Haran before fully obeying God's call to Canaan. Eventually he did learn that when God tells us to let something or someone go, He always has good reasons for it, and it's always in our best interest.

We must be careful that we don't think that, just because certain people were of great help to us in times past, we should keep depending on them for the rest of our journey. God often allows people to come into our lives for a season and only for a season. But sometimes things and people can become a hindrance and a distraction that keep us back from becoming the people the Lord would have us become.

We can save ourselves a lot of trouble and pain if we'll just do what God says by obeying Him completely. The writer of wisdom says, *"Trust in the LORD with all your heart, and lean not on your own understanding; in all your ways acknowledge Him, and He shall direct your paths"* (Prov. 3:5-6). We must be prepared, in obeying

God, to face persecution. Though it's not easy, we can be comforted to know that we are in His will and that He has our backs.

ISHMAEL

Another aspect that stands out to me is the Ishmael scenario. How many of us have unwanted "Ishmaels" in our lives because we didn't wait on the Lord or obey Him? David, many years later, said, *"Wait on the LORD; be of good courage, and He shall strengthen your heart; wait, I say, on the LORD"* (Ps. 27:14). God is faithful to accomplish what He has started, and He doesn't need our help— just our obedience and our trust in Him. His timing is not our timing. It doesn't matter how long we may have to wait; this one thing I know, God will never be one minute late. He will come through at the appointed time, which makes Him on time.

Many of us are trying to do and accomplish great exploits for God, but we find ourselves frustrated and falling disappointingly short. We need to stop, take a deep breath of exhaustion, and throw in the white towel of surrender to the Lord. It's time for us to acknowledge our dependence on Him and concede, "This will not be done unless You do it; I will not arrive at destiny until and unless You take me there." Ministry is God's work—He is the one who performs it, but He does so through His people. Therefore, we, as the people of God, need to stop trying to do God's work, and let Him do it through us. He needs to be the wind in our sails.

No doubt Abraham had gotten to the place where he had given up on the possibility of ever accomplishing the task that God was calling him to do in his own strength, especially when it became humanly impossible.

In the same way that the Lord waited until Abraham and Sarah were past the age of having children, He will wait until we run out of steam and come to the end of our rope—and then He'll step in. He does that so that we won't pat ourselves on the back, saying, "good job," and take the glory that belongs to the Lord. Sometimes the Lord allows His people to come up against impossible circumstances, not just to show how great and awesome He is, but to keep us humble and to keep things in their proper perspective. He's reminding us that we need Him and that He deserves all the glory! Though it's challenging, we must learn to wait on His timing for the fulfillment of His promises in our lives.

Waiting for My Promise

I knew the Lord had a call and purpose for me, but when I looked at my life, it all seemed impossible. An outrageous and disturbing criminal record was now hanging over my head. Saying I was a licensed minister, a Bible college graduate, and former valedictorian would be nothing short of blasphemy to those who knew me or had heard about me. Those who had been willing to recommend me for ministry opportunities would no longer do so. The things and people that I previously could fall back on to propel me into the purpose God had for me were not there anymore.

No longer can I look to myself with all the different gifts I may possess, any more than Abraham could look to himself or Sarah to have children. What God had promised was now up to God in Abraham's story; and I believe the same goes for me.

If I was ever going to come out of this mess, it would not and could not be accredited to me, to my will power, or to anything else. I was too shattered to put myself back together, and the job was too big and too messy for most to want to get involved. Though there were a few faithful saints who committed themselves to being there for me, I couldn't really look to them for the healing that my soul was crying out for; only God can put a shattered heart back together. There was no one to turn to but God. God doesn't mind getting His hands dirty or having His reputation scrutinized by sinners. That's what He did when He came to dwell among people; He became a friend of sinners and tax collectors and then died on the cross for them. Only God can claim the glory in my story.

As seen in Abraham's story, God is still faithful and able to do in you and me that which He has promised, even when we may think it's too late. If I had any reason to believe God had given up on me, I would have given up on everything, including God. What's the purpose in living for God when God could care less about me? On the contrary, I was persuaded that God was going to see me through. My desire is not just to live, to exist; I want to live my life for God and to be used by Him—fulfilling His purpose for my life. I was, with God's grace, able to encourage myself in the Lord and wrote this song to sing to myself:

I WILL NOT QUIT!

Vs. 1) If I fall, I will rise up again and stand tall. Jesus didn't say I was perfect; but faith in His blood has made me righteous. He has made me available for every good work. There is still much more for me to do and achieve. I will press to take hold of that which Jesus Christ has taken hold of me for.

Chr.) How can I ever quit when God is not through with me yet? He didn't bring me this far to say that's all—no, no, no, no, no. There is no limit to what God

will do in me, through me, and for me. By the grace of
God, I will not quit!

Vs. 2) When troubled waters are all around me, and I
can't swim to save myself, I will cry out to Jesus for help!
He will hear and answer my cry. With His outstretched
arm I'll be saved from the storm. This one thing I
know, if God doesn't calm the stormy sea, He'll stay in
the boat with me.

Brig.) I will not quit! I will press! Jesus Christ is not
through with me yet.

BECOMING A WITNESS

This song strengthened my resolve to trust in the Lord and
to make myself available to Him so He could use me right there
in prison. I was not just telling the inmates and guards that I
was a Christian; I was boldly doing it. They were all shocked and
could not believe me, but their response was legitimate considering the overall context. A saint should not be suffering in prison
like I was. If it's for obeying the Lord and doing what is right,
then yes—but not because of doing something wrong and sinful
(see 1 Pet. 4:12-16). Unfortunately, I was a saint who had sinned
and was suffering because of it.

The only way I was able to break through and witness effec-
tively to the other inmates was to share the not-so-popular side
of the great heroes of the Bible. I wasn't trying to make myself
look good by making the saints of old look bad; nor was I trying
to make them look bad to start with. That wasn't my aim. But by
showing the inmates how some of the greatest saints in the Bible
sinned and struggled with weaknesses, I was giving them hope

in the gracious and forgiving God of the Bible. I wanted them to know that, even if they'd been sinners all their lives and had committed some of the most horrible crimes, there was still hope for them too to be forgiven and born again—becoming saints.

That was my goal, and it's the message I want to keep declaring to those who are still behind bars and those who are outside of the prison walls. My deep desire and prayer to the Lord is that He will open up doors of opportunity for me and the message of this book to go into the prisons and proclaim the glorious light of the liberating Gospel of Jesus Christ to let others know there is still redeeming grace at Calvary.

CHAPTER 8

RAHAB'S STORY

From Prostitution to Salvation

 And you He made alive, who were dead in trespasses and sins (Ephesians 2:1).

I, Rahab, must admit that my reputation was not among the most desirable. I was well-known in the city of Jericho, but not because of something good. I was a prostitute. With no husband or children, I was free to do whatever I wanted to do, and we did not have any religious or civil guidelines or standards that strictly forbid such a lifestyle. It wasn't the best thing to do, I must confess, but I did it anyway. The good news, however, is that the latter part of my life was by far much greater and fulfilling than the former. Through the goodness of Almighty God, I went from being a prostitute to a member of His covenant people and an inheritor of His promises.

Did I enjoy my lifestyle as a prostitute? I did not. I felt used, abused, and dirty! Numerous nights I cried myself to sleep. I didn't feel good about the way I was living. Sometimes I wondered if I would ever break free from this lifestyle. I had dreams of one day getting married and having children. But my situation kept condemning me and pulling me back from my dreams.

I concluded that no man would want to marry a prostitute like me. I had been with so many men; I didn't think I could be on any man's list for a potential wife. It's the delight of every man to marry a virgin, and I was far from it. Furthermore, if I were to get married, I would be faced with the dilemma of whether or not to reveal my past.

Two Spies

When the two Israelite spies came into Jericho, I immediately knew they were visitors because I had never seen them before and they looked different. As they came closer to me, I tried to make myself irresistible and made sure they saw me. They came over to me and were indeed captured by my flare and beauty—so I thought.

Our conversation was fairly normal and courteous; so I invited them to my house. Then to my dismay, they revealed who they were, what they were about, and finally and most disappointingly, that they were not interested in me! They were God-fearing men who were about God's business (see Josh. 2:8-21).

To them, I was the best or easiest candidate to take advantage of. But I did admire these men deeply. They were like famous heroes who came up close and personal. I felt honored to be in their presence. These two men had witnessed a supernatural deliverance by the awesome hand of God. Most likely, as children, they had seen the plagues in Egypt (see Exod. 7–12). They ate of Heaven's delicacies (see Exod. 16); heard the voice of God audibly (see Deut. 4:10-14,33); saw God's presence in the form of a cloud (see Exod. 13:21); walked through the Red Sea on dry ground (see Exod. 14); witnessed the subduing of great kings and their kingdoms (see Num. 21; Josh 2:8-11); and received the law and precepts from the very mouth of God (see Exod. 20; Deut. 4:10-14). We were terrified of the Israelites and their God!

All the surrounding nations had heard about the Holy God of Israel, that He was fighting for them and had selected a special plot of land for them. I quickly realized that the gods we were serving could in no way be compared to this sovereign God of Heaven and earth who was on Israel's side. Unlike many in my country, I fell in love with the unfolding story of the Israelites and their God. I didn't want to find myself fighting against what I knew was inevitable—that is, the conquest of our land. I didn't want to be on the losing side. All my life I felt like I was losing out on something greater. This was what stirred up my faith in the God of Israel for a new and better beginning and legacy.

It happened that the king of Jericho heard that strange men from among the children of Israel had come into the city to spy out the land and were lodging in my house. So the king sent guards to my house to arrest the spies, but I hid them on the roof. I told the guards that they were not there. I didn't deny the fact that they had come into my house, but I did deceive them and tell them they'd already left. "Pursue them," I said, "and you may overtake them." As soon as the guards went through the city gates in pursuit of the spies, the gates were shut behind them (see Josh. 2:4-7).

If what I had done was ever found out, my life would have been in jeopardy. But my faith was bold, and I knew I was doing the right thing. So without delay, before the spies could fall asleep, I went up to them and said:

> *I know that the LORD has given you the land, that the terror of you has fallen on us, and that all the inhabitants of the land are fainthearted because of you. For we have heard how the LORD dried up the water of the Red Sea for you when you came out of Egypt, and what you did to the two kings of the Amorites who were on the other side of the Jordan, Sihon and Og, whom you utterly destroyed. And as soon as we heard these things, our hearts melted; neither did there remain any more courage in anyone because of you, for the LORD your God, He is God in heaven above and on earth beneath. Now therefore, I beg you, swear to me by the LORD, since I have shown you kindness, that you also will show kindness to my father's house, and give me a true token, and spare my father, my mother, my brothers, my sisters, and all that they have, and deliver our lives from death* (Joshua 2:8-13).

The spies were grateful for what I had done for them, and they accepted my request. We made an agreement that I would not reveal their mission to anyone. I would bring all my family into my house when the Israelites came to conquer the land, and I would make sure I hung a scarlet thread in the window to be a visible sign to distinguish my house from all the others. Whether or not I did these things would determine whether or not they would have to live up to the agreement (see Josh. 2:15-21).

So it was that after we made an oath between us, I let them down through the window on a scarlet thread. I told them to go to the mountains and remain there for three days before they continued on their journey. So they did. After three days the pursuers returned, having searched throughout the entire region without finding the spies. As a result, the people of Jericho became even more fainthearted and were in dread of the Israelites. So they fortified the city walls like never before. It was completely shut up so that no one went out and no one came in (see Josh. 6:1).

THE FALL OF JERICHO

When the children of Israel came to Jericho, they pitched their tents outside the city walls beyond the archers' reach. As they began walking around the city once every day for seven days, many of the people in the city were making fun of them, while others wondered what it meant. The priests carrying the Ark of the Covenant, and except for the men who were blowing the trumpets, no one made a sound.

I did, however, feel confident in whatever was going to happen because of the agreement I had made with the spies. Every so often I would go to the window just to make sure the scarlet thread was still there. I was filled with anticipation.

Then on the seventh day, the Israelites marched around the city seven times, and on the seventh time, all the people made a great shout, and the walls of the city began crumbling and fell to the ground. I was in shock! Miraculously and thankfully, my house was spared, at least for the time. Then the Israelites charged into the city, killing everything that moved.

Before long the two spies whom I had protected came to my house, and my family and I went with them to their camp. From that day we became a part of the children of Israel. Unfortunately, we were the only ones who came out of Jericho alive, and it was because I chose to believe in the God of Israel. Not only was I saved from the destruction, but I was welcomed into the people of Israel. I even ended up marrying a God-fearing man named

Salmon, and together we had a son named Boaz (see Josh. 6:22-25; Ruth. 4:21; Matt. 1:5).

RAY'S REFLECTIONS AND INSIGHTS

Rahab's story makes me think of the problem of the sex industry in our present age. It is a problem with which I am well acquainted, but which I now carry a great burden to fight against.

There have been times in my Christian walk when I knew within myself that my life wasn't right before the Lord. I was going to church, singing in the choir, playing the drums, and so on, but there was a war raging inside of me. This is how Peter put it: *"Beloved, I beg you as sojourners and pilgrims, abstain from fleshly lusts which war against the soul"* (1 Pet. 2:11).

I didn't feel good about myself, and at times I was miserable. I knew who the Lord had called me to be, but I was nowhere close to it. Whenever I made one step forward, it seemed as if I made two steps backward. In that season of my life, I was very tempted to leave the Church. Maybe if I left the Church, I reasoned, I would be able to go on a self-searching voyage through which I could get my life together and then come back.

I can honestly say that I was sincere in my efforts to walk in the Spirit and to live for the Lord in every way. Unfortunately, sometimes we (myself included) pack on too many do's and don'ts, trying to be the good Christian according to our own efforts. But sometimes we can be so sincerely wrong—going about things the wrong way! That was exactly what I was doing. Have you ever been sick and tired of being sick and tired? I was there. But where was I going to go? I realized that the devil wanted to isolate me so that he could totally destroy my life. So I decided that the best place for me to be was in the house of the Lord.

Vows to the Lord

Eventually, I got so serious and determined to get things right that I ended up making vows to the Lord (and I meant every word I said) with full knowledge of how serious making vows to the Lord is (see Deut. 23:21-23; Eccles. 5:4-5). I thought it would be a way to invite God to search my heart—to see how deeply I wanted to live my life for Him so that no sin would reign in my mortal body that I should obey its lusts (see Rom. 6:12)—and help me. I often didn't live up to my vows. These times brought many tears and much frustration to my life as I would, almost hesitantly, yet earnestly, go back to the Lord to repent of my sin or the breaking of my vow and to seek His merciful forgiveness for my foolishness.

I remember praying a prayer like this: "Lord, You know, and I know that I'm not living the way You would have me to. My heart is not right before You, and I'm tired of coming back to You, asking forgiveness over and over again. Why am I not experiencing lasting victory? Take a look deep down inside of my heart and see how much I love You and desire to do Your will. Why am I doing what I don't want to do and not doing what I need to do? Lord, only You can make me right. I will not stop coming into Your house; You are going to have to strike me down right in there. I am trusting in You to deliver me and make me who You want me to be. Please help me."

The Word of God says, "...*faith comes by hearing, and hearing by the word of God*" (Rom. 10:17). My reasoning was that, if I kept going to church and continued hearing the Word of God, something was being planted inside me through which I would be able to exercise my faith and believe God for complete victory. I told the Lord that I would go to my grave still trusting in Him to deliver me.

My situation was somewhat similar to what Samuel declared to the children of Israel.

> *Then Samuel said to the people, "Do not fear. You have done all this wickedness; yet do not turn aside from following the LORD, but serve the LORD with all your heart. And do not turn aside; for then you would go after empty things which cannot profit or deliver, for they are nothing. For the LORD will not forsake His people, for His great name's sake, because it has pleased the LORD to make you His people"* (1 Samuel 12:20-22).

I felt like if I left the church I would actually become worse and may not return. All along in my heart, I knew that somewhere, somehow, the Lord had to deliver me because I could not enter into my promise with the weight of hypocrisy and with a stronghold of sin. I couldn't tell how or when He was going to do it, but I knew He was going to do it—even if He had to allow me to go through the refiner's fire, and that He did.

THE SEX INDUSTRY

With regard to the sex industry, today there are prostitutes and so-called "porn stars" who outwardly give the impression that they're so happy, proud, and peaceful. But deep down inside, many of them are lonely, hurting, ashamed, and disgusted with the prison they find their souls in! Many of these women and men give their lives to this degrading practice because they're addicted to sex and are paid a great deal of money.

Regrettably, some of these "porn stars" don't have any shame; because they have no morals, they boast about their practice. Their consciences have been seared with a hot iron (see 1 Tim. 4:1-2). They have become desensitized to sin. As if they created themselves, they feel as though they can do whatever they want with their bodies without any consequences or accountability.

Perhaps this is because so many accept the theories of evolution and the Big Bang—which tell people that they came from apes, not the careful design of a loving Creator. But to take the Creator out of the picture means that there is no true purpose to our existence. It is void of destiny and has no sense of trademark accountability, traceability, and reputation to live up to. Everything is by chance, and chance is not purpose.

What or *who* we believe in has a lot to do with our worldview— our belief system, morals, and ethical practices. If people believe they came from monkeys, then they'll act like they came from monkeys, while trying to be good at it and thinking they're fulfilling their destiny and purpose.

I am not trying to write these people off from hope and saving grace. God certainly does not. This book is not about condemnation, but about the glorious hope we have in God's salvation in spite of our sins. Nonetheless, we must be aware of the empire of this industry and the fact that it's pretty much out of control—or should I say, taking control. Not only are these practices sinful, but they're destroying too many families. This is no doubt the goal of the enemy.

Some of these women, unfortunately, are forced into prostitution by "pimps." Others get sucked into it because of the sexual abuse they've experienced in their childhood. Still, for many, it's all about the money. They figure they can take the easy way out and avoid any kind of hard work or studying to get a degree in an honorable profession. They may say something like, *Why take on student loans to go to college for three or four years when I can get into prostitution or the pornography industry and make more money than teachers and doctors?* Unfortunately, they are being deceived, not knowing that the *"love of money is a root of all kinds of evil"* (1 Tim. 6:10). The devil will give them the world, with all its sinful pleasures, to make them travel hell's road, and then he'll steal their souls.

LAWLESSNESS

As seen in Rahab's story, prostitution has a long history. What makes it even more sad today is that sinners are placed on pedestals and are viewed as celebrities and role models— "idols," by virtue of their sinful acts or "achievements." It is ridiculous and shameful that the pornography industry, with its porn stars and many other sinful entertainment fields, has become so glamorized! Evil will always be evil, but today evil is being elevated to the status of good, and much good is being trampled underfoot as evil. But God's Word doesn't change, and it's the standard of good and evil.

Second Timothy 3:13 states that *"evil men and imposters will grow worse and worse, deceiving and being deceived."* The Bible also says, *"because lawlessness will abound, the love of many will grow cold"* (Matt. 24:12). People are becoming more and more lawless, not just in regard to biblical precepts, but also in relation to human laws. What the Bible is actually saying is that evil and immorality will hit unprecedented levels as the last days unfold and that such will be the moral atmosphere into which Christ will return.

Today a lot of people go on as if they have nothing to hide, as if nothing is private or sacred to them—especially in the pornography industry. They are even bolder, performing all sorts of sexual acts with numerous people and sometimes in the most disgusting ways.

In addition, numerous women are selling their talent in the music industry by performing almost naked! They do this because "sex sells." So even if a beautiful young lady can't really sing, all she has to do to "make it" is to be as nude, provocative, and tempting as possible! This, by the way, is not a general stereotype, but it does happen. Instead of a woman feeling ashamed to see her half-naked body on television and billboard posters, she may instead feel a sense of advantageous pride and fame. "My image was chosen to be on such and such a magazine," she says. And sadly it gives her a false sense of value.

Even teenage girls are dressing as though they want to show as much as they can while not showing everything—leaving the rest for others to explore in their fantasies. Like I've said, I am not stereotyping all young women, or older women for that matter; not every girl who wears a short skirt does so to show her legs or to turn heads. Likewise, not every guy who wears a sleeveless shirt or goes completely shirtless does so to show biceps or six packs in order to impress.

I don't believe you'll disagree with me when I say that many times both men and women wear certain clothes to send a message or to seek a desired response, though it may not always be in an unhealthy or negative way. This is seen most clearly on many television shows and in many magazines. The same person who may dress appropriately for an interview may turn around and dress for attention at a club party.

Am I being hypocritical by criticizing the pornographic industry when I used to look at its images? I don't think so. Once I was under its grip; I was overpowered by it. I kept my eyes open when deep in my spirit I wanted to shut them and quit looking at porn. But now it does not have control over me. I am free! Because of my experience, I have become outspoken against it. I know there is nothing positive or Christian about it (even if a husband and wife watch it together). I've seen its evil in my face.

I'm like a former drug addict who is encouraging people, especially the younger generation, to stay away from drugs. After being under the grip of the sex industry and seeing firsthand how it can destroy you, your family, your finances, your health, and so forth, I want to spare you the trouble if possible.

God can deliver us from whatever oppressive and addictive habits and lifestyle we may have. He delivered Rahab from prostitution, and He can do the same today with those who are in the sex industry. If at anytime I seem to sound harsh about certain issues or groups of people, my endeavor is not to do so void of grace. I'm a grateful recipient of God's grace, and it is that grace that I do not want to leave out of my story, regardless of the people and their issues being addressed. God looked beyond my fault and saw my need; He's just as willing to do the same for others, and so am I. But at the same time, God didn't embrace sin and ungodliness in order to love the sinner. My endeavor is to do the same, with the hopes that my message will help some find freedom from the trap and help some escape the trap altogether.

Faith for Righteousness

The second aspect of Rahab's story that stands out to me is faith. Often, when we think of faith, we think of Abraham. But the Lord did not see the work of Rahab's faith any differently than that of Abraham. Abraham believed God, and He accounted it to Abraham as righteousness (see Gen. 15:4-6). Rahab also believed God, and He accounted it to her as righteousness too. So regardless of the fact that Rahab was a prostitute and lied in order to exercise her faith in God (to protect the spies), she was not disqualified from the list of the righteous saints (see Heb. 11).

Let's look at this issue further. When Moses sent the 12 spies to spy out the land of Canaan, ten of them brought back a bad report. But the Lord considered their report not just bad, but evil. This was because their report was in opposition or contradiction to what God had previously said and promised. God had promised to give them the land and to drive out the inhabitants before them. But when they saw the reality and the challenge of the situation, they shrunk back from the promise (see Num. 13; 14).

In truth, what they were doing was declaring that God wasn't God enough to handle it. In their minds, the situation was greater than His ability to bring the promise to pass, and, therefore, the situation was god. Whatever or whoever is greater than God ought to be God. If there is a situation that is beyond God's ability to transform, then that situation would prove to God that "it" is god above Him.

Paul declared through the revelation of the Holy Spirit:

Therefore God also has highly exalted Him and given Him the name which is above every name, that at the name of Jesus every knee should bow, of those in heaven, and of those on earth, and of those under the earth (Philippians 2:9-10).

God gave Jesus His name because Jesus came from God and was God. So if there was or is a name above His name, He would be under subjection to that name.

When you cannot make sense of what God has said or is saying, obedience is still required—you must still believe. God had said to Noah, *"Whoever sheds man's blood, by man his blood shall be shed…"* (Gen. 9:6). Nonetheless, God commanded the Israelites to completely destroy all the people of the land that they were to possess. It was God's way of bringing judgment on the people because of their wickedness (see Exod. 23:20-24; Gen. 15:16).

There are some things in the Bible that aren't so easily understood. For example, Jacob lied to his father to steal his brother's blessings. The means might have been questionable, but the end was ultimately God's will (see Gen. 25:19-26; 27). There is also the fact that after Isaac was so bluntly deceived by Jacob, he still ended up blessing him a second time without even confronting him about his deception (see Gen. 28:1-5). Where is the "rightness" in this that God would not even address it? Rahab went from being a prostitute to being righteously justified in the eyes of the Lord because of her faith in Him. She became a Jew and ended up marrying a God-fearing man named Salmon. Together they had a son, Boaz, who became the great grandfather of King David, which means that Rahab was part of the lineage of Jesus Christ (see Ruth 4:21; Matt. 1:1-6).

Truly, this is an example of the Lord's goodness and grace. Even though Rahab was not a descendant of Abraham by birth, but was a heathen, a sinner by nature and practice, and a prostitute, God used her as an example to show that He loves all people of all races and that we can go from whatever lifestyle we find ourselves in, to salvation in Him. His hope is available to everyone!

WITHOUT SIN

When the woman who was caught in adultery was brought to Jesus in John 8, He showed mercy and not judgment. The men who brought her wanted to test Jesus so they could find something to accuse Him of; they also wanted to stone her to death. But Jesus said, *"He who is without sin among you, let him throw a stone at her first"* (John 8:7). It didn't take long for them to look into their own hearts and lives and realize that they too were not only sinners, but hypocritical sinners at that!

If she was caught in the very act of adultery, according to the law of Moses, both she and the man (or men) were to be stoned—the punishment was not just for the woman (see Lev. 20:10). You can sin by doing what you're not supposed to as well as by failing to do what you're supposed to. It's called the sin of omission.

Wisely, Jesus didn't say, "He who has never committed adultery, cast the first stone." He knew that they were not all adulterers, and therefore, whoever was not guilty of adultery would have been justified, based on the challenge of the question, to stone her. Instead He said, *"He who is without sin...."* He knew that all people are sinners in some way and are, therefore, unfit to condemn each other.

They had to acknowledge that though none of them may have sinned outwardly and so embarrassingly, they were not void of sin. The only person who could legitimately judge her with righteousness and true justice was Jesus because He was sinless and had no need to be partial or merciful while considering His own imperfections or the possibility that His time of judgment and the need for mercy would come. And He offered her mercy.

Jesus warned the Pharisees and all who trusted in their own self-righteousness not to judge and focus on the sins of others when there is even greater sin in their lives (see Matt. 7:1-5). He shattered the Pharisees' expectations and beliefs when He said, *"...Assuredly I say to you that tax collectors and harlots enter the kingdom of God before you"* (Matt. 21:31). I know that the loving hands of God can reach the vilest of sinners if they cry out to Him and put their trust in Him.

It's not what you do that will get you to Heaven or send you to hell, so to speak; it's who you are. I was born in sin and lived out my sinful nature in many different ways. The same is true of all of us. But the day I put my faith in God, He clothed me in His righteousness, and I became a saint.

Are you a sinner or a saint—are you a child of God? John 1:11 says, *"He came to His own, and His own did not receive Him. But as many as received Him, to them He gave the right to become children of God, to those who believe in His name."* Humankind has the choice as to whether they will remain children of wrath and of the devil—sinners through the Adamic nature—or whether they will become children of God, inheriting salvation through Jesus' redemption, adoption, and nature of righteousness.

THE GREATEST ISSUE

The greatest issue facing humankind today is the same issue that Rahab was faced with—faith. Sin is not the greatest issue people are faced with because Jesus dealt with sin on the cross and removed its eternal consequence. He took the sin of the world upon Himself when He went to the cross, and the judgment of God was poured out on Him who carried the sin. There, on the cross, the justice of Almighty God was met and satisfied.

Herein lies the issue:

*For God so loved the world that He gave His only begotten Son, that whoever **believes** in Him should not perish but have everlasting life. For God did not send His Son into the world to condemn the world, but that the world through Him might be saved* (John 3:16-17).

A lot of people read that Scripture and stop right there, but listen to what the following verses say:

> **He who believes in Him is not condemned; but he who does not believe is condemned already,** *because he has not believed in the name of the only begotten Son of God. And this is the condemnation, that the light has come into the world, and men loved darkness rather than light, because their deeds were evil. For everyone practicing evil hates the light and does not come to the light, lest his deeds should be exposed* (John 3:18-20).

To believe is not just to believe and go on living however we feel—like unregenerate heathen. We believe in the existence and laws of gravity so we don't jump off skyscrapers pretending like we can fly. The result would be fatal. Likewise, when we believe in God and accept the redeeming work of Jesus on the cross, we must live our lives in accordance with our beliefs—we become children of God, which means He has called us into relationship in His family and into consecration—holiness.

Believing is only the initial stage that brings about reconciliation so that the relationship with God may begin, but it must continue on. To believe is to be progressive in faith, practice, and relationship—moving from thoughts and feelings to obedience and action, moving from glory to glory. It is almost equivalent to getting married and saying your vows. After a wedding, the husband and wife certainly don't go about their separate business and homes; they become one and cleave to each other.

Jesus paid the price for sin—a price that we could not pay. We owe a debt that we could not pay, and He paid the debt that He did not owe. Therefore, the greatest issue is whether or not people will acknowledge and accept the fact that Jesus died for them and paid their sin debt. Not one man or woman has ever walked the face of the earth, except Jesus, who never sinned and therefore doesn't need forgiveness.

The man of wisdom, Solomon, said, *"For there is not a just man on earth who does good and does not sin"* (Eccles. 7:20). The people who do not believe in Jesus as the atoning sacrifice of God are already condemned and are walking around with a stamp on their hearts, invisible to the naked eye, saying, "I am guilty of sin."

John 16:8-9 says, *"And when He has come, He will convict the world of sin, and of righteousness, and of judgment: of sin because they do not believe in Me."* I believe, if there is one question God will ask humankind when they stand before Him, it will be this: "What did you do with My gift, My Son—Jesus of Nazareth?" This question has already been played out when Jesus was crucified. It is so profound and eternally significant to all humankind that its echo could be heard all the way back to Adam and Eve—before Christ. It also resounds to this present day and will continue to do so till the end of the age.

THE CROSS DEMANDS A RESPONSE

There were three crosses on Calvary that represent three words: the one in the middle, where Jesus was crucified, stands for *redemption;* the one on the right, *reception;* and the one on the left, *rejection.* The cross in the middle demands an answer, a response to the gift and question of redemption. "Will you believe Me and receive My gift, or will you doubt Me and reject My gift?" Humankind is given the freedom to choose eternity in Heaven with God or eternity in hell with the devil. God has done His part, and now the ball is in the court of every person's heart.

Consider these eternally inspired words spoken directly and indirectly by Jesus and the Holy Spirit through His saints,

Most assuredly, I say to you, he who hears My words and believes in Him who sent Me has everlasting life, and shall not come into judgment, but has passed from death into life (John 5:24).

For I am not ashamed of the gospel of Christ, for it is the power of God to salvation for everyone who believes... (Romans 1:16).

If you confess with your mouth the Lord Jesus and believe in your heart that God has raised Him from the dead, you will be saved. For with the heart one believes unto righteousness, and with the mouth confession is made unto salvation (Romans 10:9-10).

For whatever is born of God overcomes the world. And this is the victory that has overcome the world—our faith. Who is he who overcomes the world, but he who believes that Jesus is the Son of God? (1 John 5:4-5)

He who overcomes shall inherit all things, and I will be his God and he shall be My son. But the cowardly, unbelieving, abominable, murderers, sexually immoral, sorcerers, idolaters, and all liars shall have their part in the lake which burns with fire and brimstone, which is the second death (Revelation 21:7-8).

In the last Scripture, the unbelieving is listed among the other categories of sinners. None of the sins that are listed are unpardonable sins. However, if people choose not to believe in God and the atoning work of Jesus, God will not forgive their sins. Peter, speaking of Jesus, declared in Acts 4:12, *"Nor is there salvation in any other, for there is no other name under heaven given among men by which we must be saved."*

ONE WAY

God has not and will not make any other channel for salvation. Even ancient Israel, with their sacrificial system, particularly the Day of Atonement, received forgiveness because blood was shed. It was symbolic, a foreshadowing of what the true Lamb of God, Jesus, would one day accomplish once and for all.

The children of Israel only had one means to protect their firstborn from the death angel in Egypt—killing a specified animal that was without blemish and putting the blood on the doorposts and on the lintels of their houses (see Exod. 11-12). In the wilderness, when snakes bit the people because they sinned against God, the people cried out to Moses, who took the case to the Lord. The Lord told Moses to make a bronze snake and put it on a pole; whoever was bitten by a deadly serpent, and looked at the bronze snake, would be healed (see Num. 21). To refuse to do what the Lord commanded and reject the solution He provided was to choose to die in arrogance and rebellion—essentially suicide.

In these two examples, God did not provide an alternative, and so it is with salvation. God has provided the sin offering—Himself. It doesn't make any sense that God would become a man and allow Himself to go through such horrible crucifixion if He knew that there were at least one or two more alternative ways for us to be forgiven of our sins, reconciled to Him, and on our way to Heaven. No, Jesus is the only way.

You need to know that God is able to do in you and through you what you cannot do for yourself. Rahab was living in prostitution for most of her life, but when she put her faith and life in God's hands, He changed her and gave her His salvation. He can turn your life around. It doesn't matter how bound you are; He can break the chains.

If you think you're too deep in the pit, His outstretched arm can reach down there and rescue you. If you think your darkness has surrounded you so much that He can't even see you, He still can. He is the light of the world. Cry out to Him and allow Him to come into your situation. He can turn your life around in spite of what you have been through, what you have done, and where you find yourself today. He wants you to experience the fullness of His salvation. You don't deserve it, nor can you earn it, but that's how great His awesome grace and unconditional love are for you.

The Word of God summarizes Rahab's story in this way:

By faith the harlot Rahab did not perish with those who did not believe, when she had received the spies with peace (Hebrews 11:31).

You see then that a man is justified by works, and not by faith only. Likewise, was not Rahab the harlot also justified by works when she received the messengers and sent them out another way? (James 2:24-25)

Truly Rahab's story testifies of the scope and power of God's mercy and redemption for those who choose to believe.

CHAPTER 9

JUDAH'S STORY

When Sin Puts on Shame

 Righteousness exalts a nation, but sin is a reproach to any people (Proverbs 14:34).

I, Judah, was a child of promise and purpose, the fourth of 12 sons who became known as the 12 tribes of Israel. I was proud of my ancestral heritage coming from Abraham, Isaac, and Jacob, my father. I knew my family was at the initial stage of something great and that the culmination of it would be universal. Though I had the family's destiny in mind, I also wanted a break from everything that was going on in the family. I wanted to explore my own desires for a change. This was the road that led me down the path of my unrighteousness that included a very disgraceful sin and its shameful covering.

As chosen people, we were commanded to stay within the family lineage and not to intermarry with the other people of the land and surrounding nations because of the promise. The Lord had promised our great grandfather, Abraham,

> *I will make you a great nation; I will bless you and make your name great; and you shall be a blessing. I will bless those who bless you, and I will curse him who curses you; and in you all the families of the earth shall be blessed* (Genesis 12:2-3).

And later, the Lord said to Abraham,

> *Blessing I will bless you, and multiplying I will multiply your descendants as the stars of the heaven and as the sand which is on the seashore; and your descendants shall possess the gate of their enemies. In your seed all the nations of the earth shall be blessed, because you have obeyed My voice* (Genesis 22:17-18).

GETTING RID OF JOSEPH

As time went by, the Lord visited my brother Joseph in the form of dreams, and we hated him as a result of his dreams—because they indicated that we would one day all bow down to him. We thought of killing him, but we later changed our minds and sold him into slavery (see Gen. 37). This changed everything in our family.

We killed a goat kid and took Joseph's specially designed coat of many colors, which our father had made just for him. We covered it with the blood and made a few rips here and there in it. It was all a part of our plan to cover up what we had done. So we took the coat to our father and presented it to him, pretending like we didn't know who it belonged to. Our father immediately recognized it and, presuming that Joseph had been devoured by a wild beast, broke down in bitter tears and anguish.

It was a painful sight to behold. We had never seen our father in such agony before! We were all grieved by our father's pain—knowing in our hearts what we had done and that we were lying about it in his face! And on top of that, some of us began shedding tears too, to show sympathy with our father so it would seem like we missed him and didn't have anything to do with his "death." It was the most sickening feeling of guilt and falsehood I'd ever felt!

If God were to call our spirits to the testimony stand, our lies would have all been exposed. *"The spirit of man is the lamp of the LORD, searching all the inner depths of his heart"* (Prov. 20:27). Though our lips were lying, our spirits wanted to tell the truth, but we suppressed it.

Not one drop of our tears was genuine. It was all a show, and God knew it too. The money that we got from selling our brother felt like poison in our hearts. No wonder things began to look and feel depressing all around us. Our brother was gone, and our father was never happy again because his favorite son was dead (so he thought). Since things were not going well at home, I left.

Sojourn in Canaan

I departed from my father's house and went to the daughters of Canaan. Shortly after I got there, I fell in love with a Canaanite woman. Not long after we met, we got married. I wanted someone and something to bring some form of happiness to my life, at least for a while, and to give my mind a break from my family affairs. In the process of time, my wife and I had three sons, Er, Onan, and Shelah (see Gen. 38:1-5). In the past we had refused to give our sister, Dina, in marriage to Shechem the Hivite, not just because he had raped her, but because he was not of our race (see Gen. 34). But there I was marrying and having children with a Canaanite.

Before long my firstborn grew up and was ready for marriage. So I went and found a beautiful wife for him named Tamar. But Er was obsessed with just about everything that was evil, and he became evil and wicked. So the Lord ended his life in the prime of his strength. According to the custom of the day, Onan then became Tamar's husband in order to raise up an heir or descendant for his dead brother. Onan knew that if Tamar became pregnant the child would not take on his name, but his brother's. Thus, whenever he had sex with her, he would emit his semen on the ground.

At first I couldn't understand why Onan would do that. Suddenly it dawned on me that maybe it was because Er was so wicked. Onan had despised him and had not wanted his brother to live much longer, let alone have children. But that's only my assumption. Nonetheless, the actions of Onan were considered as evil in the sight of the Lord, and the Lord killed him just like his brother. It's very likely that Onan fooled himself into thinking that his narrow-minded, inconsiderate, and unloving actions toward his wife and even his dead brother in no way compared to his brother's sins and, therefore, were not worthy of God's judgment. He was wrong. God killed him. And there I was, grieving the death of yet another son.

At that point, I told my daughter-in-law that she should go back to her father's house and remain a widow until my youngest and last son, Shelah, was old enough to marry her (see Gen. 38:11-14). But I wasn't truthful or faithful to my word. I was afraid that my last son would suffer the fate of his two brothers. So I waited and waited in hopes that she would forget about my promise and become inpatient and marry someone else. But she didn't.

TAMAR'S REVENGE

It was during this waiting period that my wife died. This definitely gave me an even greater reason to want to hold on to my last hope—my son. After mourning my wife's death and receiving some degree of comfort, I decided to go up to my sheepshearers with one of my friends. Someone heard of my plans and passed it on to my daughter-in-law, Tamar. After she was informed about my plans, she became furious and thought of how she could get even with me. I hadn't given her my son to be her husband, even though he was of the age. So she got dressed and prepared herself like a harlot. She didn't do it to make a living from it or to get any and everybody's attention. She did it specifically to catch me; she knew I was vulnerable.

As I journeyed on the road to Timna, I saw a woman on the street dressed as a harlot with her face covered, and she made sure I saw her. So I went over to her and asked her if I could sleep with her. She replied, *"What will you give me, that you may come in to me?"* (Gen. 38:16). I didn't have any money, so I told her I would send her a goat from the flock the next day. But that wasn't good enough for her—she wanted a pledge. So I asked her, *"What pledge shall I give you?"* (Gen. 38:18). She replied by asking for my signet (signature ring), bracelet, and the staff that was in my hand. That was the trade-off. She felt comfortable with it, and we slept together (see Gen. 38:15-18).

What I did not know was that the prostitute I had slept with was my own daughter-in-law! She became a prostitute for a day and sucked me into her deceptive arms. She knew all along what she was doing. But since all this information was not yet revealed to me, I sent the young goat to her with my friend just like I had promised. I wanted my pledge back from her.

Now the story began to get even more shameful. My friend could not find the woman. He went back to the same location over and over again. He asked the men who were from that neighborhood about the prostitute who was openly by that area, but they were not aware of any prostitute in their community. Surely, if there was a harlot in the vicinity, the men would have at least noticed her.

But like I said before, she wasn't there day in and night out for men to take advantage of her or the other way around. She wasn't even there for the money. She timed my journey, and like a spy, she planned her move precisely and covertly and was successful. My friend continued his earnest search for her, but to no avail. He came back and gave me the news. Then I said, *"Let her take them for herself, lest we be shamed; for I sent this young goat and you have not found her"* (Gen. 38:23).

Three months later I got news that my daughter-in-law had played the harlot and, on top of that, was pregnant. How dare she do such a thing! I was outraged and insulted—it was a disgrace to the family! So I pronounced judgment on her and commanded that she be brought out and burned! I said to myself, "She does not deserve to live. She's a harlot!" So we had her brought out in the open to be burned (see Gen. 38:24-26). By this time, I had despised her so much I didn't even want to see her face again!

But then, to my disbelief and shame, she sent a messenger to me saying, *"By the man to whom these belong, I am with child. Please determine whose these are—the signet and cord, and staff"* (Gen. 38:25). I was embarrassed and humiliated! My sin had stripped me naked, and now shame was clothing me. I was covered in shame! Everybody could see the shame of my sin. The evidence against me was both convincing and convicting, and there was no way I could pretend the items weren't mine. I had to acknowledge before all the people that they were mine, which also implied that I was the father of the "harlot's" child. Talk about shame—it doesn't get much worse than that!

In spite of it all, I was still reluctant to confess that I had sinned. Instead I said something like, *"She has been more righteous than I, because I did not give her to Shelah my son"* (Gen. 38:26). I admitted that I hadn't lived up to my word, but I didn't, at first, admit that my behavior was sinful. The sentence to burn Tamar was overturned because I was no less of a sinner than her, and I would have been deserving of the same judgment too. As much as I wanted to abandon her, I could not. However, our relationship was very moderate. Never again did we have an intimate relationship, even though she became the mother of my twin boys, Perez and Zerah (see Gen. 38:27-30).

CHOSEN IN SPITE OF MYSELF

After many years, there was a great famine in the entire region, so we went back to my father's house. This famine led us down to Egypt where we were eventually reunited with our brother Joseph and later went to live with him in Goshen (see Gen. 41-50).

The most incredible part of my story is that God chose me and my family above my brothers, even after the ways in which I sinned. Just before my father Jacob died, he pronounced his blessings on us individually, including Joseph's two sons. And the greatest blessing came to me. Here's a part of that blessing,

The scepter shall not depart from Judah, nor a lawgiver from between his feet, until Shiloh comes; and to Him shall be the obedience of the people... (Genesis 49:10).

Through my genealogy, namely Perez, the son whom I fathered in harlotry, the Messiah would come. The Lord also chose my family to go up first in the conquest of the Promised Land, and He chose my allotment in the city of Jerusalem to be the dwelling place of His holy temple. I often wondered why God didn't choose Joseph instead. After all, he was more perfect and blameless than all of us—plus what he did and went through would certainly make his descendants the model candidates. Or God could have chosen Benjamin—young and innocent, or Asher, Dan, Gad, Issachar, or one of the others.

But He didn't. Instead, by choosing me, God was demonstrating His awesome power and grace to show that He can and will use the weak as well as the strong, the poor as well as the rich, the unwise, as well as the wise, the highly esteemed as well as the lowly esteemed, and so forth.

RAY'S REFLECTIONS AND INSIGHTS

I am always struck by the danger of judging others that is portrayed in Judah's story. Onan, most likely judged his brother Er, and he died for his presumption. Judah too nearly passed judgment on Tamar when he was just as guilty as her. Putting different degrees to evil and sin, overall, is unwise. In Ezekiel 18:4 the Lord says, *"Behold, all souls are Mine; the soul of the father as well as the soul of the son is Mine; the soul who sins shall die."* Lying can send you to hell just as much as committing murder can.

Some believers will be surprised when they get to Heaven. They will see some murderers, adulterers, fornicators, prostitutes, rapists, child molesters, sorcerers, homosexuals, sex offenders, thieves, drunkards, and so on. They might wonder, "How did you get here?" And every one of those saints will answer the same way, "I confessed my sins and repented, and the Lord forgave me."

These same believers may be even more surprised to discover that some of the people who went to church every Sunday, directed the choir, sang in the choir, taught Sunday school and children's church, served on the deacon board, preached the Word of God, sang on the worship team, and ministered in the music department are not there. Then they will wonder, "How come brother or sister so-and-so isn't here?"

And the angels will reply, "They had a form of godliness, but they denied the power" (see 2 Tim. 3:1-5). They practiced covetousness, backbiting, and slandering. They lusted, sowed discord among the brethren, were prideful, hated others in their hearts, showed injustice and partiality, drew near with their lips, but kept their hearts far away, had idols of worship in their hearts, and were unforgiving toward others. Most importantly, they did not confess their sins, repent, and receive the Lord's forgiveness. They chose to practice and remain in their lifestyles of sin; thus their names were erased from the Lamb's Book of Life (see Rev. 3:4-5).

FINDING GOD-ESTEEM

The shame that Judah and his brothers must have felt while watching their father mourn the "death" of Joseph, knowing they had sold their own brother into slavery and then deceived their father, resonates with me. I know what shame feels like. As I was in jail and reflecting over my life, I found that I no longer had any self-esteem. I was no longer egotistical, nor did I have a good opinion of myself anymore. I had just brought about the greatest embarrassment of all time to myself and my family! Self-esteem was no longer a part of my vocabulary.

I realized that self-esteem is always based on something—our clothes, our cars, the kinds of jobs we have, the levels of education we have, the houses we live in, our physical appearance, our integrity, and on and on. The fact is, even though we may have good reasons to have good self-esteem, if and when we sin disgracefully, the integrity and trust we've accumulated over the years either will be suppressed or will completely disappear.

When all my self-esteem was gone, I learned that to be an overcomer in the valley, I needed "God-esteem." Only God-esteem was going to deliver me from the condemnation of self-esteem. God-esteem is seeing ourselves the way God sees us—knowing that we are who God says we are and that we can do what He says we can do. It is seeing ourselves through the eyes of God. Unlike God, who doesn't need any objective reason to feel great about Himself, we often do.

The attributes that God possesses within Himself (see Galatians 5:22-23, though He's not limited to these) are more than enough for Him to glory in Himself and could be viewed as God's own "God/Self-esteem." The Lord says in Isaiah 46:9-10,

> ...For I am God, and there is no other; I am God, and there is none like Me, declaring the end from the beginning, and from ancient times things that are not yet done, saying, "My counsel shall stand, and I will do all My pleasure."

Only God can declare those things with the power within Himself to back them up. But let's look at God-esteem as an inheritance that we have received because we are joint heirs with

Christ (see Rom. 8:14-17), possessing a transformed and renewed mind.

When we become saints, our opinions don't really count anymore; only the truth of God's Word counts. If that isn't true in our hearts, when circumstances affect our emotions and change our opinions about ourselves, how will we be able to stand? Paul said,

> *I have been crucified with Christ; it is no longer I who live, but Christ lives in me; and the life which I now live in the flesh I live by faith in the Son of God, who loved me and gave Himself for me* (Galatians 2:20).

If you are a sisterly saint who struggles with your physical appearance, you need to stop beating down on yourself to fit into the image of what the world calls "beautiful" or "sexy." You need to understand that God's approval of beauty is not based on your weight or lack of it, nor does your body have to be a specific shape with Hollywood's stamp of approval. Hollywood doesn't know anything about the beauty of a godly and virtuous woman like the one described in Proverbs 31.

Beauty is from within—the gentle attitude and condition of the heart (see 1 Pet. 3:1-6). Therefore, regardless of your size, shape, or any other factor regarding worldly beauty and appearance, you should still be able to say, *"...I am fearfully and wonderfully made..."* (Ps. 139:14). This, of course, does not mean that you and I are not supposed to take care of our bodies, but just that our image does not determine our value.

Some of the "celebrities" who pride themselves on living in the box the world and the entertainment industry has made for them, though they look beautiful on the outside, may at closer examination turn out to be on par with Jezebel! Would you call her beautiful? The Bible sure doesn't (see 1 Kings 21:1-24; Rev. 2:18-20).

If we build our houses on the sand of self-esteem (the world, things, people, and their opinions), when the storms come, and they will come, our destruction will be inevitable. But if we build our houses on the rock (God and the eternal truth of His Word), when the storms come, His Word and His mighty power will sustain us.

Second Corinthians 5:21 says, *"For He made Him who knew no sin to be sin for us, that we might become the righteousness of God in Him."* This was a trade-off. My righteousness is from God and of God, not of anything that I have or haven't done that would give me reason to have a good opinion of myself. *"He who glories, let him glory in the LORD. For not he who commends himself is approved, but whom the Lord commends"* (2 Cor. 10:17-18).

A VISION OF THE KING

When you get a vision of the Lord, like Isaiah did, you can't help but throw your self-esteem out the window. Isaiah, when he saw the Lord enthroned in His holiness, cried out and said, *"Woe is me, for I am undone! Because I am a man of unclean lips, and I dwell in the midst of a people of unclean lips; for my eyes have seen the King..."* (Isa. 6:5). I wonder what Isaiah's opinion about himself was before he had that vision? Regardless, afterward he had only eyes for God. Think of Peter. Certainly his self-esteem would not have been able to lift him out of his pity-party pit after he denied Jesus three times. He felt like an unworthy, weak failure. He needed to see himself with God's eyes.

When others or our own self-esteem fail to love or like us, we must know that God Almighty still loves us unconditionally.

If God loves us, He's telling us that we are precious to Him and worthy of His love—not deserving of it, but worthy or worth it. If we, His own creation, were not worth His love, then He would not have died for us. We must learn to say to ourselves, "If God was willing to shed His blood on a wooden cross on Calvary for me, then it means He really and truly loves me." This is reason enough to love ourselves even when circumstances are telling us to do otherwise.

If we are able to love ourselves, then we can love others too. It is only possible to love our enemies through God's eyes. The reason so many of us still carry the baggage of self-esteem is because we compare ourselves with each other and not the true standard—God. So when a fellow saint has fallen and sinned disgracefully, we pack on more "self-esteem" because now we feel "holier." But are we really? Listen to these two Scriptures in the writings of Solomon. *"Let another man praise you, and not your own mouth; a stranger, and not your own lips"* (Prov. 27:2). *"Do you see a man wise in his own eyes? There is more hope for a fool than for him"* (Prov. 26:12).

David, when he was going through a rough time in his life, said to himself, *"Why are you cast down, O my soul? And why are you disquieted within me? Hope in God; for I shall yet have reason to praise Him, the help of my countenance and my God"* (Ps. 43:5). David could not strengthen himself because he was weak, and he could not hope in himself either because there was no hope in him. He had to hope in the Lord and seek strength from Him.

Just like David, I knew my esteem would be of God, and not of me. I was and am the redeemed of the Lord, and I was going to still say so, regardless of what anyone was saying about me or even of what I thought about myself. Some may call me a monster, a predator, a liar, a hypocrite, a sinner. I've repented. I traded in the shame of my self-esteem for God-esteem, knowing that I was still a saint, forgiven of the Lord, and still called by Him—even though I had sinned and was in prison.

CONFIDENCE IN GOD

I know what it's like to feel ashamed and to know that there is no power within me to free me of it—except the power of the Holy Spirit. If I had not known my position in the Lord and seen myself the way the Lord sees me, I could have very easily lived the rest of my life in the ocean of guilt and shame, walking around with my head hanging down—bowing to the devil's will.

Hebrews 10:35 encourages us not to *"cast away your confidence, which has great reward."* This confidence is not in ourselves, but rather in God. I can testify that I don't always feel like traveling the straight and narrow road (the faith walk of Christianity). None of us do. Sometimes it gets tough, and often the trouble, persecution, and difficult situations we experience have nothing to do with our sins, but are just trials that come to refine us according to First Peter 1:6-8; 4:12-16.

Though I understand my justification, I do not and will not deny this shameful period of my past. What I have done and will continue to do is to trust in the God of my salvation, while continuing to seek forgiveness and reconciliation wherever and whenever possible, especially where it's most needed.

I know that I must also be prepared as to when and how to share my story with my children. When they're old enough, should they read this book and seek daddy's "in person," verbal explanation, how will I deal with stirring up so much more hurt? It will not be easy, and that's a milestone for which I will most certainly have to seek the Lord for His grace and wisdom. I know God will make His grace abound toward me in all things because He has failed to fail me yet.

ACCORDING TO MY FUTURE

A powerful truth is that God doesn't just see us based on the past or present, but on the future. For example, when the Angel of the Lord called Gideon, He said to him, *"...The LORD is with you, you mighty man of valor"* (Judg. 6:12). Gideon replied, *"O my Lord, how can I save Israel? Indeed my clan is the weakest in Manasseh, and I am the least in my father's house"* (Judg. 6:15).

Here Gideon, who wasn't a warrior, was being challenged to see himself the way the Lord saw him—as a warrior. He thought he was weak and insignificant because of his situation and position, but the power of God esteemed him out of his situation and self-esteem (see Judg. 6:11-7:25).

Maybe Judah wrote himself off; maybe he didn't. But regardless of how he saw himself, God had a future for him and his tribe, and it wasn't because Judah outdid his brothers in acts of righteousness.

Even though the Lord has dealt with my issues of guilt and shame, I still struggle with them from time to time. It's not because I have doubts about the Lord's forgiveness, but because I have an adversary, the devil, who tries to bring my past back in my face, tries to make me drown in the ocean of guilt and shame. This is a spiritual battle I have to be vigilant in, and God is giving me the grace to do just that.

Even though Judah took on the fatherly responsibility of his twin sons, it's possible that from time to time as he watched them play, he had to fight off the memory of the sinful act that brought them forth, regardless of the fact that they may have been a blessing and brought him much joy.

To be honest, I'm not sure if 30 years will change by any vast degree the way I feel with regard to my own crime. I have thought to myself that maybe, if I was telling my story 30 years after the fact, I would see and say some things differently. That may prove to be true, but I do know that my experience would not permit me to say a lot of things differently than how I've said them in this account.

I will always regret and denounce my behavior and any like it! I will always be ill at ease about the victim. As a matter of fact, every time I see or hear of a news report similar to mine where a female was harassed or assaulted, regardless of the degree, a light bulb of concern and condolence goes off in my head for the victim—and for the victim of my own story.

A Light in the Darkness

I've always loved that God chose Judah and gave his family line a great blessing even though Judah had messed up so much. Like the other stories in this book, it gave me great hope that God would not only forgive me, but also use me for His purposes on this earth. As I said earlier, after landing in prison, I didn't have anything to be prideful about; my pride was completely shattered, but I held on to my confidence in God. It was in this confidence that I was able to be His minister and soldier within the enemy's camp. Before long I was connected to the chaplain, through whom the Lord gave me great favor. She gave me a Bible and told me to keep it. Previously, I had had a small Gideon's Bible. However, I had lent it to another inmate with a list of Scriptures to read, but he never gave it back to me. (Later I found out that he, along with some of the other inmates, had torn out the pages to make cigarettes.)

With this new Bible, I started reading, studying, and sharing the Gospel with many inmates. Some had never heard the Gospel; some had never even heard of Moses or David. The more I preached and prayed for all the inmates, the more I began feeling the joy of the Lord strengthening me (see Neh. 8:10).

From time to time inmates would come into my cell to hear me share the Gospel. On a few occasions, some of them would say, "I feel so much peace when I'm in your cell." I knew it wasn't my presence or peace they were sensing, but the peace that comes with the presence of God who was with me and in me.

Eventually, the chaplain brought me down to her office to get to know me a little better—not to find out why I was there, but to learn whether or not I was a true saint who had sinned or a sinner who was seriously pursing salvation. So I shared with her who I was and my calling in the Lord. I didn't share with her what had gotten me into jail because the Lord had not given me the grace and strength to share it at that point when I was still dealing with so many issues.

I asked her if it would be possible to go into the chapel to play the piano for a while, and she said, "Yes." This took me to another level, as I was able to try to put into music what my words could not express! I was able to pour out my heart with tears on the piano! This became a regular thing for me. Even during regular lockdown periods in the afternoons, the chaplain would come and get me and allow me to go into the chapel to worship and play music. O how this was a blessing to me! I had the chapel all to myself to cry out to God. In many ways, I felt like Joseph who had received favor from God in prison.

LEADING WORSHIP

Before long, the chaplain suggested that I lead in a time of praise and worship on Sunday mornings and evenings before she ministered. I gladly said yes. Soon the chapel started to get packed with inmates. It started to overflow so much that it became a problem. A sign-up sheet had to be sent around to the different units for inmates to sign up in advance if they were coming to church. The chaplain would also make sure that those who showed sincere interest in God and the Bible had first preference.

Not long after I started leading praise and worship, she brought in a few different guys to me, one by one, who said they could play an instrument. I was fairly knowledgeable and familiar with playing the drums, piano, and the bass guitar, all of which were in the chapel—plus an acoustic and electric guitar that I couldn't play very well. So I would take the guys and have jam sessions with them to determine whether or not they could play. The chaplain accepted whatever and whomever I recommended to her.

Within a short period of time we had a full band. We had a bass player, acoustic and electric guitar players, a drummer, and me on the piano. No, they didn't have to be born again and baptized in order to be a part of the worship team—this was prison policy. The hope was, however, that in coming to church, being in the presence of the Lord, and hearing the Gospel preached Sunday after Sunday, God would "arrest" their hearts so that they would come to the liberating truth of the Gospel of Jesus Christ.

On a regular basis we would have practice time, and whenever there was a big function in the gymnasium with a guest speaker, the correctional band, as we were called, would start off by doing the praise and worship and a few specials. As a result of this ministry role, I became known to most, if not all, of the inmates and guards in the prison, and again the Lord gave me favor with them. The chaplain and I became good friends, and she would often have me meet with some of her guests.

Inmates were turning over their lives to the Lord and committing themselves to turn from their life of crime to grow in their relationship with the Lord. Some of the guys who came just to get away from their unit had completely changed and were now sincerely seeking the Lord. And hearing news from the chaplain of some of the guys who got out and who were now part of a church brought much joy to me.

THANKFUL FOR FREEDOM

In the midst of all of this though, I had the shocking and unbelievable revelation that some of the inmates were already planning what their next crime spree was going to be! One of them even suggested that I join him. I could not believe my ears! Never in a million years would I allow myself to go down a path that could potentially land me right back in jail—not after what I had gone through, before and since. As a matter of fact, if I were to ever stand before a judge again, facing criminal charges, with my already reproachable criminal record, I wouldn't want to even try to picture the outcome.

I'm not saying that any given judge would use my past to convict me in the present even if I'm innocent. I do have confidence in the justice system, even though it is evident that people are sometimes wrongfully convicted. However, there's a reason why the prosecutor brings up criminal records, as in my case, where the judge asked for a copy of my records, even though I didn't have one. The reason behind it was to see if I'd been in trouble with the law before.

This would give him an indication of whether or not I was a lifestyle criminal who didn't fear the justice system. In my case, it could show him that I made some foolish choices contrary to my character that got me in a mess. Sometimes one mess-up is messy enough to cause people not to see the light of the sun again (thankfully this was not the case for me). But God's grace can still give them the opportunity to see His Son (Jesus), who cannot be denied visitation beyond walls, barbwires, and guards.

Don't you guys enjoy freedom? I thought to myself. *Don't you have a purpose for living?* Amazement, disbelief, and questions flooded my mind. I saw it with my own eyes; guys who were released ended up back in prison within a few weeks and sometimes even days. I can actually say that there are indeed people in prison who don't care one iota if they keep going back there or remain there. Thankfully, there are some who are genuinely remorseful, have gotten the message, and are purposely making changes in their lives for the better.

Observing the patterns of sin in many of these men made me even more thankful, not only for God's mercy, but also for His empowering grace to change. I knew He still had a purpose for my life and that He could make me into a man worthy of the calling (as He does for all of us who follow Him wholeheartedly).

UNABLE TO HIDE

Another aspect of Judah's life that I could relate to was his inability to hide his sin. His choice to sleep with the prostitute caught up with him in the most humiliating way. In the same way,

I could not hide from the shame of my sin. My wrong actions were on display for all to see.

Like Adam and Eve, shame was the by-product of my sin. After they sinned and were ashamed of their nakedness, they made themselves coverings from the figs. Though there wasn't anything sinful about their nudity or the fact that they sought to cover it up, they couldn't hide from the knowledge of their sin, which resulted in them being ashamed of their nakedness. Though they covered themselves with leaves, the knowledge of their sin still placed a shameful covering on their naked consciences.

But God was merciful to them and made tunics of animal skin and clothed them, which meant that God shed the first blood on earth (see Gen. 3:7, 20-21). Here you see that from the very beginning God was establishing, through the shedding of blood in sacrifice, the seriousness of sin, the consequence of it, and the price of redemption. The theological implications of this initial sacrifice are of great significance and worthy of further study.

OUR NEED FOR CLOTHING

From a biblical and historical understanding, it is evident that the introduction of clothing for humankind was a symbolic representation to cover up both the spiritual and physical nakedness of man. If Adam and Eve hadn't sinned, there would not be any shame in our nakedness and, thus, no need for clothes. Furthermore, our minds would not be so tempted and polluted concerning "skin" and "figure."

The clothes of sinners are their shameful unrighteousness, but the clothes of saints are God's righteousness. David, the psalmist, said in Psalm 132:9, *"Let your priests be clothed with righteousness, and let Your saints shout for joy."* Isaiah, from a different context, also said,

> *We are all like an unclean thing, and all our righteousnesses are like filthy rags; we all fade as a leaf, and our iniquities, like the wind, have taken us away* (Isaiah 64:6).

Here Isaiah was equating our own self-righteousness, not to mention our unrighteousness, with filthy, dirty rags—shameful clothing.

Now, considering the fact that shame is a spiritual diagnosis of a symptom resulting from sin, it can only be dealt with spiritually. Shame that's based on objective factors, like the kind of work we do or the car we drive, is for the most part within our power to deal with and does not arise from a sinful act. Only God can deal with the deep shame that comes from the guilt of sin.

Let's look at the showdown that took place in Heaven's court that Zechariah saw:

> *Then he showed me Joshua the high priest standing before the Angel of the LORD, and Satan standing at his right hand to oppose him. And the LORD said to Satan, "The LORD rebuke you, Satan! The LORD who has chosen Jerusalem rebuke you! Is this not a brand plucked from the fire?" Now Joshua was clothed with filthy garments, and was standing before the Angel. Then He answered and spoke to those who stood before Him, saying, "Take away the filthy garments from him." And to him He said, "See, I have removed your iniquity from you, and I will clothe you with rich robes." And I [Zechariah] said, "Let them put a turban on his head." So they put a clean turban on his head, and they put the clothes on him. And the Angel of the LORD stood by* (Zechariah 3:1-5).

In place of earthly garments, whether filthy or clean, God will give pure white garments as a symbol of the righteousness of His saints. John saw something similar in the Book of Revelation:

"Let us be glad and rejoice and give Him glory, for the marriage of the Lamb has come, and His wife has made herself ready." And to her [the Church] *it was granted to be arrayed in fine linen, clean and bright, for the linen is the righteous acts of the saints* (Revelation 19:7-8).

The Bible often uses clothing as a metaphor in terms of righteousness, majesty, holiness, strength, honor, shame, sin, and so forth. Therefore, from this standpoint, the Laodicean church was encouraged to acquire white garments from the Lord to cover their nakedness. The Lord said,

I counsel you to buy from Me gold refined in the fire, that you may be rich; and white garments, that you may be clothed, that the shame of your nakedness may not be revealed; and anoint your eyes with eye slave, that you may see (Revelation 3:18).

USED BY THE LORD

Like the Laodiceans, we all need to be clothed with the Lord's righteousness. If I have to be perfect for God to use me, He will never use me because I'm not perfect. It is also a lesson to those who may be stronger, more honorable, wiser, and so forth, not to think more highly of themselves than they ought. Jeremiah, speaking as the oracle of God, said it best:

"Let not the wise man glory in his wisdom, let not the mighty man glory in his might, nor let the rich man glory in his riches; but let him who glories glory in this, that he understands and

knows Me, that I am the LORD, exercising lovingkind-ness, judgment, and righteousness in the earth. For in these I delight," says the LORD (Jeremiah 9:23-24).

First Corinthians 12:1-11 also talks about various spiritual gifts that the Spirit of God distributes to each one individually as He wills. God can use the church janitor as much as the pastor. The usher can speak a word of wisdom or knowledge to another member or even the congregation at large as much as the overseer can. A Ph.D. or M.A. doesn't make us more mature, qualified, or spiritual in the Kingdom of God than the people who love the Lord with all their hearts, souls, minds, and strength—who are obedient to the Lord and who spend time with Him, seeking His face and doing His will.

I remember one day when we were under lockdown for a few hours and I began singing *Amazing Grace* in my cell. As soon as I was through singing, a few of the guys in nearby cells asked if I could sing it again and a little louder this time. So I did.

After the lockdown was over, one of the guys came to me and said, "I was having a terrible headache, but by the time you were done singing, it was completely gone." To some, that wouldn't be a big deal, maybe even coincidence. But to me, at the time, it was God confirming His hand upon me and His presence with me. And as He did, my spirit was lifted and strengthened.

God did not say to me, "Ray, I can't use you while you're in prison. You have to wait until you get out, get back in the church, and repent again before the whole congregation; then I'll be able to use you again." No, God did not say that to me. Neither do I believe He's that limited. Once we repent, it opens the door for God to work in and through us for His glory and for our good.

So many people are trying to put God in the self-made box of their minds. But look what the Lord declared through His prophet Isaiah:

> *Let the wicked forsake his way, and the unrighteous man his thoughts; let him return to the LORD, and He will have mercy on him; and to our God, for He will abundantly pardon. For My thoughts are not your thoughts, nor are your ways My ways... (Isaiah 55:7-8).*

If God uses the wicked to do His will, certainly He will use His saints who have momentarily sinned against Him and repented, though they may still be in the situation caused by their disobedience. Humankind cannot make a box to contain God in any way, shape, or form. He does not act according to our ideas or expectations, or according to what we think is right or fair. Only God's Word and His integrity restrain Him.

CHAPTER 10

RAY'S STORY, PART 3

God Is Not Limited by Limitations

 Behold, I am the LORD, the God of all flesh. Is there anything too hard for Me? (Jeremiah 32:27)

Without any question, I knew the Lord had called me on a journey toward the purpose and plans He has for my life. But I found myself at a juncture where I was forced to take a deep look at my life and ask myself some questions. I had to acknowledge that I had fallen in sin many times and was presently at the bottom of rock bottom—in the sense of how sinfully and drastically I had fallen and the limitations that it had now placed on me.

LEAVING PRISON

Before I move on with the remainder of my story, let me first bring my prison experience to a close. The night before I was released, the guards moved me to a new unit of the jail; it was some form of policy, it seemed. They brought me to a cell and locked me inside. But the guys on that unit were still free to walk up and down the corridor of that unit. So from time to time they would gather at my cell to talk with me.

I had always worn my wedding ring and had never felt or been threatened for it, except for one occasion where one of the inmates was persistently begging me to let him see it. However, that night I felt that not only was I in danger of losing my ring, but that my safety and life itself were in danger!

As the inmates gathered outside my cell, our conversation went from casual to uncomfortable. Suddenly, they weren't just asking to see my ring; they were demanding that I give it to them! I tried to calm them down and told them that it was my wedding ring and was precious to me. But they didn't care one bit. I was praying so hard in my heart for God's protection, that He would send His angels to protect me! I didn't need to feel His protection; I needed to see it—really, literally see it! The guys were determined to get my ring, and I was determined to keep praying and trust in God.

The guys took a mop stick off of a mop and began showing me how they could put a knife on it and reach me (I was all the way at the back of the cell). "O Lord God, help me, I pray! If I die in this place, You will not get any glory, because I will die in my mess and then how will You be able to turn it into a message? Lord, I'm trusting in You. My life is in Your hands..." I prayed.

All of a sudden, it was time for lockdown, and the guards shouted that it was time for everyone to get into their cells. I don't think I've ever taken such a deep sigh in all my life! But before the guys left, they made sure to threaten me, saying that they had friends on every unit and could inquire from them and find out where I live and come after me if I said anything to the guards about what had happened. My last night in prison was the worst night of all, at least from a physically threatening standpoint!

After they departed from my cell door, I began looking around at the cell walls. All I could see were drawings of the ugliest looking creatures and "monsters" that someone who was "serving the time," instead of letting the time serve him, had created. I, on the other hand, had purposed to use the time to study God's Word more, witness to others, write numerous songs, and so forth. I had to, with God's help of course, find a way to make that season of my life count—and not be wasted. I'm sure I wasn't the only one who had such purpose. I learned from my prison experience that we can just exist in time, or we can be living in time—using time as the fuel on the journey to fulfilling our purpose. Some people are strolling along in life, just barely surviving; others are enjoying life—the journey of living. Moses understood this truth and said it best in his prayer in Psalm 90:12, *"So teach us to number our days, that we may gain a heart of wisdom."*

GOING HOME

The next morning, bright and early, I was released from prison and was picked up by a fellow saint who was a volunteer at the prison; he had volunteered to pick me up and take me to the airport. As I got on the plane with the ticket my wife had purchased for me, I was joyful in my spirit to be free again, but I was still conscious of the fact that there were many challenges awaiting me. I knew, however, that God was making me an overcomer because He is not limited with regard to my limitations. He also assured me that He was with me and would not allow me to stay under and further go under, but to go over.

In going back home, I had to make amends with my wife and humbly and graciously ask her to forgive me! I am so grateful to God for my wife, Suzanne Moore, the Christ-like woman whom He has blessed me with! She had the gracious love of Christ in her and was able to forgive me and help me in moving on. I'm forever grateful to her for helping me when I needed it the most and for not leaving me when I made leaving easy.

When I read David's words, "...*Oh, that I had wings like a dove! I would fly away and be at rest*" (Ps. 55:6), I could feel a sense of what he was talking about—the feeling of flying away from all your troubles, pain, hurt, and challenges to a place of rest or a new beginning. I felt like flying away—not that I would do it, but I felt like it and wished that I could do it.

Going Back to Church

The court required me, upon my release, to go for psychiatric evaluation and counseling, along with other demands. The government had a system set up to attempt to rehabilitate me, to reintroduce me into society, and hopefully to prevent me from reoffending. However, when I looked to my former church, all I saw was rejection. I was turned off and decided not to force myself into a denomination that wouldn't even extend a helping hand to a wounded saint.

Now, looking back, I see that my response to the church was not all that right and proper either. I could have and should have been more humble in pursuing their forgiveness with an apology and so forth. Though I did pursue their forgiveness with an apology, I could have been a lot more humble in my approach. But seeing arms folded instead of arms open wide didn't give me much motivation and comfort in wanting to approach.

Not all the saints were like that to me, but some were, including leaders. I was and still am thankful for the saints who were there for me all the way through. Some of them wrote and encouraged me in prison, and some made themselves available for me to call them even though they knew it would be a collect call.

A DIFFERENT CHURCH

I decided I wasn't going to let any opposition or negativity stop me from going to church. So the first Sunday after I got out of prison, I went to church with my wife and daughter, my parents, and my mother-in-law. This was a new church because my wife had moved from the city where I committed my crimes. Yet this new town wasn't that far from the church we attended before we moved so I could attend Bible college.

After the service, I was greeted by much of the congregation and the pastor, a wonderful man of God. I must admit, though, that I was uneasy as I observed the saints as they were worshiping and listening to the sermon and greeting me as a visitor. I wondered whether, if they knew what I'd done and where I had just come from, they would be so receptive of me or willing to greet me.

The pastor, however, did know because my wife and mother-in-law had shared it with him, and he had been lifting me up in prayer while I was in prison. He was more than willing to help me and told me he would like to talk with me. He said that whenever I felt like talking, I should not be fearful, but should come and talk with him. Eventually I did, and he was very gracious to me and prayed for me.

When I saw that the church needed some help in the music department, a part of me wanted to extend my musical gifts to help, but a part of me didn't. The pastor didn't ask me to be a part of it; he was using wisdom in making sure he could trust me, before slowly introducing me to a ministry role in his church. And I was not about to force myself to be a part of a church ministry, to begin with.

In the process of time, to make a long story short, I ended up playing piano on the worship team and occasionally leading the worship service. This pastor, Larry Hanford of the Word of Life Church in Camrose, Alberta, was God's vessel to help bring healing to me, with the prospect of getting back on the journey in full confidence and assurance that God still has a purpose and mission for my life. Even when my probation officer called to inform him about me, he wasn't moved by what she said because I had already shared everything with him, and he believed I was truly repentant.

Previous to this, I decided I had to confess the true intent of my heart to the justice system with regard to my crime. After I told the probation officer, she decided to tell her boss, who in turn relayed the information to the jurisdiction wherein I stood to face my charges. I was scared because I didn't know if somehow I would end up back in jail for coming clean about my motives. But I felt I had to do it. Thankfully, I did not have to go back to jail because they said that they were convinced of my motives and the court proceedings took it into consideration.

FEELING LIKE THE PRODIGAL SON

As I continued going to church, I found myself experiencing something similar to that of the prodigal son. This experience, however, did not come from the church I was now attending, but rather from some of the saints of my previous denomination and churches I'd been a part of.

The prodigal son had asked his father for his share of the family inheritance. Upon receiving his share, he went out to a far country and wasted his money on what the Bible calls "prodigal living." When all his money was gone, there arose a severe famine in the land, and he became famished and desperate. Somehow he missed this Scripture, *"An inheritance gained hastily at the beginning will not be blessed at the end"* (Prov. 20:21).

In his desperation, he went and got a job with a citizen of that country who would send him out in the fields to feed the pigs. But no one gave him anything, not even to eat. Things got so bad for him that he started eating the pigs' food! Fortunately, he came to his senses and realized that even the servants in his father's house were better off than he was. So he decided he would return home and confess that he had sinned against Heaven and his father and was no longer worthy to be called his son. Instead, he would ask his father to hire him as a servant.

When his father saw him coming from a distance, he had compassion on him, ran to meet him, embraced him, and kissed him! The father was so joyful to see his son back home that he didn't even pay any attention to his son's confession—at least at the initial welcome celebration (that's the impression the Scripture gives). The father commanded that they put the best robe on him, put a ring on his finger, sandals on his feet, and kill the best calf to have a party for his son. The father said, *"For this my son was dead and is alive again; he was lost and is found"* (Luke 15:24).

The sad part about this story, which also relates to my story, is the unforgiving elder brother who had stayed home. When the elder brother came in from the fields and heard the celebration, he inquired what it was all about. When he found out it was for his wayward brother who had returned home, he fumed, was enraged, and would not even go inside! His father went out to him and pleaded with him to come in and join the celebration. But he refused—defending his integrity and loyalty to his father. Then he accused his father of showing favoritism because, in spite of his faithfulness to his father, he had never even been given a young goat to kill for a party with his friends. He said (in my paraphrase), "But here comes your 'sinner' son who spent your livelihood on harlots, and here you are, having the biggest party for him!" (See the full story in Luke 15:11-32.)

MY UNFORGIVING BROTHER

The unforgiving brother represents some of the saints who "remained" at home, and the father represents God. However, the father's depiction of God is somewhat limited because he stayed home and waited for his son to return, whereas God comes looking for us—like He did for me in that jail cell. God is willing to leave the 99 healthy saints at home to venture out and look for the one saint who is lost and wounded because of sin—ready to be completely devoured by the enemy (see Matt. 18:10-14; 1 Pet. 5:8-9).

I found that many of the saints were looking down on me and seemed almost disappointed to see me back on the journey of Christianity. Proverbs 17:9 says, *"He who covers a transgression seeks love, but he who repeats a matter separates friends."* It seemed like they wanted me to perish in the land of my sins and affliction—like I shouldn't come back to church. It was heart-wrenching and confusing.

The Father had forgiven me and was raising me back up from the pit, yet my brother couldn't see past his selfishness to see the Father's stubborn love for me. The unforgiving brother failed to see his own selfishness and self-righteousness because he was so aware of his brother's unrighteousness. It gave him extra confidence in his own self-righteousness to be able to point out all his brother's sins. It's too easy to point the finger when the spotlight is not on us. But when the spotlight is on us, it reveals our own defects and imperfections that weren't previously so obvious; then we are forced to deal with ourselves—not somebody else in the grandstand.

Coming out of prison, I had so much to deal with—my own issues, making things right with my wife, and living with a disgraceful criminal record almost comparable in scope to the worst of crimes. There was also probation, the scars of being in prison, terrible nightmares, a worrisome concern for my victim, and so on, not to mention the question, "Will I ever get a job again?"

The last place I expected resistance was one of the first places it came from, the Church—some of my brothers and sisters in Christ. It was enough to make me just want to "home church myself" and say, "I don't have to allow myself to go through this." Some people like me may never set foot back inside a church due to abandonment from other Christians. It is much more common than we like to think, and it doesn't always relate to sin in people's lives.

Thankfully, the Lord granted me His grace to go on and reminded me that He is the Father—the owner of the house and the one who makes the final call. He reminded me of His grace and led me to Isaiah 44:22, which says, *"I have blotted out, like a thick cloud, your transgressions, and like a cloud, your sins. Return to*

Me, for I have redeemed you." I found such strength in this! God did not call me to return to a church, a worship team, a choir, or other saints. His call was for me to first and foremost return to Him.

I began to say to myself, "They're not my Father; it's not their house; it's not their livestock, robe, and ring; and they certainly don't have the final say over my life and my purpose." At the same time, however, it still hurt deeply being in the house and being aware that some of the saints were despising me in their hearts and refusing to believe that God can work things out for my good and for His glory.

The God on the mountaintop is the same God in the valley. It's also in the valley that we find the creek wherein we can see our reflections and what needs to be changed in us. God is not going to abandon us when we find ourselves in the valley where things become difficult. If anything, that's when we need Him most. Limitations and difficulties are only from our perspective, not God's. Nothing is difficult for God. After all, He only had to speak, and the world and the universe were created. God says,

> *Fear not, for I am with you; be not dismayed, for I am your God. I will strengthen you, yes, I will help you, I will uphold you with My righteous right hand* (Isaiah 41:10).

The sovereign Word of God conquered all my fears and anxieties, enabling me to press through the pain and resistance I experienced.

LEFT BY THE ROADSIDE

I wasn't enthusiastic about going back to my previous church because they wanted me to bare my soul before they were willing to help me. I felt like a man wounded in a car accident who had to provide proof of insurance before the EMTs would give him CPR. Even if he had been entirely responsible for the accident and others had been injured as well, no one would ever deny him medical help for any reason. They would give him the help he needed and then deal with the issues that led up to the accident later.

My church community didn't really show much interest in my restoration and well-being; neither did I show much effort in fitting back in again. At times I was confused and processed my thoughts based on my emotions. Sometimes I honestly didn't know if I wanted to be welcomed back or just left alone. Thus I write with some of those conflicted feelings, but also with fresh understanding because I don't want to make it seem as if I maintained a healthy, right mental posture at all times throughout my ordeal.

I've heard of situations where a man goes on a killing rampage, but is finally shot and wounded by a security guard or police officer. Upon the arrival of paramedics, they try their best to save the suspect so he can later face the justice system. The paramedics don't say, "He is going to get the death penalty, so there's no need to waste our time, effort, and medical supplies to keep him alive just so that taxpayers' money can feed him in prison—keeping him alive for death, on death row." Even if they were to think those thoughts, they still would have to follow procedure and do their job.

The Church should do the same for its members. The ministry of the Church involves being the spiritual, psychological, and even the physical responders to rescue the fallen and wounded saints who eventually must still face the spiritual justice system of discipline. Certainly there should be caution and wisdom in how to go about doing such rescue, encompassing discipline and restoration in order to protect the Church so that the Church isn't seen as a place that embraces sin, but as a place where sin is not given freedom to rule.

One of the first reassuring steps the church/leaders could have taken is a simpe reassurance that they were praying for me—as trivial as that may sound sometimes. Though the pastor and youth pastor, both of whom I had a good relationship with, had come to visit with me, the visit and effort seemed short lived. I do remember them praying fervently for me though, and I appreciated their prayer and thanked them for it. Today the youth pastor and I still have a relationship. Unfortunately, the same cannot be said about the senior pastor. Nonetheless, I'm still believing that we'll be reconciled and meet again.

I've kept the name of these churches and individuals anonymous because it's not my aim to expose anyone in any way. I still love and forgive those who I felt abandoned me for whatever reason.

THE LORD FIGHTS FOR ME

It's God's will that I overcome my rock bottom setbacks in sin and draw closer to Him to finish the race He has called me to run—regardless of whether I ever sing another song in church. That's the God of the Bible. He cares more about us than our singing, preaching, or drum-playing. He is also watching over His word to perform it and bring it to pass, both His written Word and His word spoken personally and directly over our lives.

Sometimes we think we're so close to God, but the way we treat others, especially those who are of the household of faith, shows that we are far from Him—we minister out of feelings and public opinions instead of the heart of God. Issues are issues, and people are people. The two are not synonymous, nor are they of equal value.

I was hurting and wounded, and it seemed as though some of the saints were, from a distance, throwing salt in my wounds. I had more than enough reasons, subjective and objective, to be bitter, but I knew my destiny was in God's hands and not other people's. Though some of the saints were adding more limits to my limitations, I knew that God was still greater than any limitation that was standing in my way. It was easier for me to be bitter than to travel the already difficult road to becoming better.

Even in finding a job, God was there for me. When I went in for an interview for one job, the lady doing the interview looked at my résumé and realized there was a gap in my work history. So she said to me, "What happened here? How come you didn't work during that year?" I told her, "I went through a bad experience, committed a crime, and was in jail." That was it; she didn't even ask me one more question about my work history or jail issue. She went through the rest of my résumé, asked me a few more questions of a different nature, and then gave me the job. That was God.

THE GOOD SAMARITAN

Here's what I have learned on my journey (which compared to many is not all that long since I'm still in my 20s). If you were beaten by robbers and left to die on the side of the road (like the story of the good Samaritan in Luke 10), but you received compassion from a stranger who picked you up, took you to the emergency room, and paid your medical bills, you would be likely to respond more quickly to a stranger in need of help than the person who hasn't experienced a similar downfall. In Jesus' parable, the priest and Levite who passed by the wounded man on the road didn't stop to think that one day they or a family member could also be in a similar position in need of help.

The sad part about this story is that the priest and the Levite, judging by their titles, should have been much closer to God than the Samaritan. The priest and the Levite were God's ministers to the people. The priest would have been like a pastor today, and the Levite, a privileged member of the leadership team. But it wasn't the Levite or the priest who stopped; it was an "un-churched" person.

THE POTTER'S HAND

Personally, I am thankful that one of the personality descriptions the Lord applies to Himself is that of a "Potter" (see Jer. 18:1-6). As long as I'm living here on earth as a saint, I am in the Potter's hands. I will never be perfected to the point where God will put me on a shelf, step back to admire His handiwork, and say, "It is good." The only time we won't need ongoing "touch up" is when we're perfected in His presence. We shall be like Him when we see Him (see 1 John 3:2-3).

I am always moldable. Even if the clay falls apart, the Potter is not so limited that He would throw in the towel in hopelessness. When Jeremiah was sent on a mission to the potter's house by the Lord, this is what he said:

> Then I went down to the potter's house, and there he was, making something at the wheel. And the vessel that he made of clay was marred in the hand of the potter; so he made it again into another vessel, as it seemed good to the potter to make. Then the word of the LORD came to me, saying: "O house of Israel, can I not do with you as this potter?" says the

Lord. "Look, as the clay is in the potter's hand, so are you in My hand..." (Jeremiah 18:3-6).

I was persuaded that this was my case, and this was what inspired me to write this song:

MENDER OF BROKEN PIECES

Vs. 1) Gather all the shattered pieces; don't let them go to waste. The suffering here, the pain over there, the abandonment and fear; your blunders here and there; your fame and your shame; the defeats and victories; bring them to Me, says the Lord, and surrender your all. I will use them to glorify Me and strengthen you as you grow.

Chr.) For My love for you is great; it won't leave you where you are. I will raise you up and make you whole. Broken pieces and sin-ruined lives are why I died and rose again. Don't let your past hold you prisoner anymore.

Vs. 2) I am the Potter, and you are the clay. Who you can be is in My hands. It doesn't matter what you've done, where you have been, or what you've been through; what people know about you, think and say about you, won't affect My plans for you. You're in the palm of My hands. I refuse to let you go. I will do for you what no one else can. I am able to make all things new.

God never changes and is not limited by our limitations. If we say that God is limited, He is only limited with regard to the truth because He cannot lie. He is limited to victory because He cannot fail or be defeated. He is limited to His infallibility because He cannot sin. He is also limited to His immutability because He cannot change. But in respect to circumstances of hopelessness or human impossibilities, God is more than able to effect change. I cannot of my own effect the change, but like John said, "...*He who is in you is greater than he who is in the world*" (1 John 4:4).

THE LORD IS MY SHEPHERD

My assumption was that the saints would support brothers and sisters who had sinned disgracefully, but who got back up, shook the dust off their feet to move on, and made things right with the Lord—rather than continually looking down on them like they're possessed sinners who have sold their souls to the devil, received the mark of the beast, and can no longer be saved.

Nobody is moved or inspired by a quitter. As humans, we pride ourselves in seeing someone rise above challenges to overcome things that could have easily been an insurmountable obstacle, whether in the area of health, physique, education, athletics, background, race, experience, and so forth. Unfortunately, when someone is at that crossroad of insurmountable obstacles, we so often position ourselves to be an additional challenge, making the quitting option more appealing. It's not rocket science to figure out that, more often than not, quitting is easier than standing your ground to fight, especially when the support you're looking for is not there.

Since Almighty God is my Father, I am persuaded that He is my defender and sustainer and that He who has begun a good work in me will complete it until the day of Jesus Christ (see Phil. 1:6). The saints did not begin a good work in me, nor did such and such a denomination—God did. At the same time, I know that God's helping hand often comes through His people. So I cannot and will not seek to isolate myself from my brothers and sisters as if I don't need them, regardless of the past.

The Word of God, with all the messages, acts, and different stories, was written for *"doctrine, for reproof, for correction, for instruction in righteousness, that the man of God may be complete, thoroughly equipped for every good work"* (2 Tim. 3:16-17). We should learn from examples inside and outside of the Bible. Romans 15:4 says it even better, *"For whatever things were written before were written for our learning, that we through the patience and comfort of the Scriptures might have hope."* The Scriptures should set the standard for how we treat each other.

God has given to the Church pastors as shepherds of the flock, but if those shepherds fail to do what is right (they are human like the rest of us), Almighty God, who is the Chief Shepherd, will not abandon His sheep to the ruin of the under-shepherd. *"The LORD upholds all who fall, and raises up all who are bowed down"* (Ps. 145:14). When leaders in the Church do not respond with loving care for the flock, we can be confident that the Lord is still caring for us and protecting us from harm.

THE JUDGMENT SEAT

As you can imagine, my intention was not to make an exhaustive list of my sins; there are too many, and I can't remember them all either—let alone the secret sins of the heart. I've sinned in many other shameful and regrettable ways. However, the sin that highlights my story was the one that truly broke me in every way imaginable and brought me through the fire on my knees! Like the Prodigal Son, I had to deal with the fact that I'd sinned against God (Heaven), while at the same time breaking the law of the land (humanity).

I am aware of the fact that some people may never pardon me, but God has already pardoned me. If people were to pardon me while God does not, then I'd be hopeless and in big trouble—eternally guilty and condemned to hell. On the other hand, if God pardons me while people refuse, I am only guilty in the eyes of people here on earth, and this is only temporary and cannot affect my eternity with God in Heaven, nor my peace and relationship with Him here and now.

Many who have never, and may never, break the law of the land, may be fornicating, lying to or about each other, living in homosexual relations, worshiping idols, getting drunk, practicing witchcraft and other forms of divinations, coveting, lusting in their hearts, and committing adultery. They will never get a criminal record based on these things. If, however, they do not turn from their sins against God (Heaven) by repenting, receiving God's forgiveness, and being reconciled to Him, they will all forfeit the grace that could have been theirs.

The day these people stand before Almighty God, the Judge of all mankind, at the great white throne judgment (see Rev. 20), He will declare His verdict against them: guilty—sinners. But when the saints (who have all sinned, but walked in repentance and accepted His pardoning grace) stand before Him at the judgment seat, He will acquit them and declare His verdict for them: not guilty—saints (see 1 Cor. 3:9-15; 2 Cor. 5:9-10). This judgment of the saints actually has more to do with being rewarded for our service to the Lord than it does with determining whether or not we're sinners or saints. It's a judgment free of condemnation.

THE SICK NEED A DOCTOR

Show me the vilest offender or the world's greatest sinner, and I'll show you the God who forgives. I have fallen and sinned so many times that, if God refuses to forgive, Heaven is not attainable for me. If any of us have fallen even once, if God refuses to forgive us, Heaven is beyond our reach. There are no sinless saints in Heaven, only forgiven ones. Keep in mind that sin is both doing what you're not supposed to do and failing to do what you are supposed to do. Psalm 130:3-4 says, *"If You, Lord, should mark iniquities, O Lord, who could stand? But there is forgiveness with You, that You may be feared."*

Many believers look at sinners and tell them, "Get your life together and then come." But that is not the teaching of Jesus. How about letting them come so Jesus can put them together? We cannot change them, nor can they bring about the deepest change that is needed in their hearts—that is the work of the Holy Spirit. We can't set them free any more than the Israelites could deliver themselves from bondage in Egypt. The doctor does not tell the sick person, "You have to deal with that sickness and get better before you can come and see me." That would be ridiculous! Let's look at what Jesus said about that: *"Those who are well have no need of a physician, but those who are sick. I have not come to call the righteous, but sinners, to repentance"* (Luke 5:31-32).

We as the Church need to stand up and be the EMS that will attend to the cry of the unsaved! Bring them in—broken, wounded, shattered, torn, bruised, bleeding, hurting, addicted, rejected, oppressed, depressed—all of them needing forgiveness, healing, and deliverance from the Lord. Whenever people are in a situation where they feel a sense of helplessness, it will often lead them to hopelessness.

One of the worst places you could ever find yourself is at the place called "hopeless." We must understand that the devil is in the business of blinding people's eyes when they're in their "caves" so they won't see the Light—the end of the darkness. Proverbs 18:14 says, *"The spirit of a man will sustain him in sickness, but who can bear a broken spirit?"* When people are broken, shattered, and hurting, only God can truly help them, though you and I may be His hands extended—the vessels through whom He works.

SPEAKING TO DRY BONES

In the vision I had of being dead to the point of skeleton-like dry bones (like the story of the valley of dry bones in Ezekiel 37), I knew the Lord was not limited by human limitations. The Lord said to Ezekiel, *"'Son of man, can these bones live?' So I answered, 'O Lord GOD, You know'"* (Ezek. 37:3). The Lord brought Ezekiel to a valley of dry bones that were scattered all over the place. Then the Lord asked him if the bones could live. The impossibility and limitation of the sight could only be changed by God alone. God commanded Ezekiel to speak to the bones, and as he did, the bones began rattling and came together, bone to bone. Then sinew, flesh, and skin covered them.

Though everything looked great, they didn't have any breath in them. Then the Lord told Ezekiel to prophesy for the breath to come, and he did. Suddenly, the breath came and entered the dead bodies, and life entered into them, and they stood up on their feet. What is a limitation to us is not a limitation to God. And what is impossible with us is not impossible with God (see Luke 1:37). Anyone looking at what Ezekiel saw would have had legitimate reasons to be hopeless because of the limitations and the impossibility of the situation. But it's not so for those who know and understand the God of the Bible—the Creator and Re-creator, the Giver and Sustainer of life, He who is Himself the resurrection of life.

In my vision, when I saw that I was dead and the Lord spoke to my spirit and told me He had a mission for me, I knew somehow He would give me life again. It was as though God was speaking to me through this Scripture because I could relate to it:

> *"I have surely heard Ephraim bemoaning himself: 'You have chastised me, and I was chastised, like an untrained bull; restore me, and I will return, for You are the LORD my God. Surely, after my turning, I repented; and after I was instructed, I struck myself on the thigh; I was ashamed, yes even humiliated, because I bore the reproach of my youth.' Is Ephraim My dear son? Is he a pleasant child? For though I spoke against him, I earnestly remember him still; therefore My heart yearns for him; I will surely have mercy on him,"* says *the LORD* (Jeremiah 31:18-20).

COME FORTH!

You may be reading this book and are yourself in a situation where you think there's absolutely no way out. Don't limit the here-and-now power of Jesus as Mary and Martha did! Though they acknowledged that Jesus was the Son of God and that their brother, Lazarus, who had died, would indeed come back to life, they did not believe in a present resurrection, but rather in the resurrection of the end of days. They had given up on Jesus because He didn't come when they wanted Him to; He didn't come when a miracle was still possible; He didn't come when change was yet realistic; He didn't come when they had strong faith; He didn't come when the dead was among the living; He didn't come when…

"...*If You had been here, my brother would not have died*" (John 11:21,32), said both Mary and Martha. Even though Lazarus was dead, Jesus told His disciples at first that he was just sleeping. What may seem like our greatest enemy and the gravest of all limitations is still within the power of God to bring about change and life. If He had showed up while Lazarus was sick, their despair would have immediately turned into hopeful anticipation for a miraculous healing and recovery, but because he was now dead, their hope was also dead—laid to rest in the tomb with their brother.

Being shut up for four days in that tomb, Lazarus' body was starting to stink and slowly decompose. Then came Jesus to the tomb in deep tears, and He said, "*Take away the stone*" (John 11:39). But Martha resisted Him because Lazarus had been dead for four days, and there would be a bad stench. Jesus reminded her that if she believed, she would see the glory of God. So they proceeded in taking away the stone. Then Jesus began praying. When He had finished praying, He cried out with a loud voice and said, "*Lazarus, come forth!*" (John 11:43). All of a sudden, he who was dead, who was rotting and stinking, walked out of the tomb bound from the crown of his head to the sole of his feet with grave clothes. Jesus said, "*Loose him, and let him go*" (John 11:44).

You may be bound from head to toe in your own form of grave clothes, shut up in a tomb of stench and rottenness where no one even wants to come too close. But I know a God whose love for you is stronger than death itself and is, therefore, not limited to whatever tomb you may find yourself in! He can loose you and let you go. He has done it for me, and He can do it for you.

I am His, and He is mine. He will hear me when I call, and I will hear Him when He calls my name—for I am His child. He knows my name, the number of hairs on my head, my thoughts from afar off, and the words of my thoughts before I speak them (see Jer. 1:5; Isa. 45:4; Matt. 10:29-31; Ps. 139:1-4; Heb. 4:12-13). My God is able to do exceedingly above all that I could ever ask or think of Him, according to His mighty power that works in me (see Eph. 3:20). The same God who saved me also has more than enough power to keep me. The same is true for you. Between here and home eternal is a journey we must walk, a race we must run with things to overcome. Persecution and trials await us, and we will experience times of weaknesses, but He promises His grace will also be sufficient for us (see 2 Cor. 12:8-10).

Just as He said to the children of Israel (who we could say are a picture of the Church in the Old Testament), He is also saying to me and every other saint who has sinned and is in need of grace:

"Come now, and let us reason together," says the LORD, "Though your sins are like scarlet, they shall be as white as snow; though they are red like crimson, they shall be as wool. If you are willing and obedient, you shall eat the good of the land; but if you refuse and rebel, you shall be devoured by the sword..." (Isaiah 1:18-20).

TRIUMPHANT MINISTRIES

Currently, the Lord has placed me in a small, young, and vibrant independent church called Triumphant Ministries in Edmonton, Alberta. When the pastor who had just founded this ministry (which the Lord had given her a vision for 17 years prior) called and invited me to be a part of the ministry, I was simply amazed! She told me that the Lord had placed me in her heart and told her to call me to come and lead the ministry. What was also redeeming about this was the fact that she had knowledge, at least to a certain extent, of my prison experience and the fact that

I'd just recently gotten out. At first, I was in awe of the reality that God was calling me to such a worthy cause when I had so many reasons to feel unworthy.

It was no coincidence that the name of this new church was Triumphant Ministries and that the Lord was making me a part of it. The Lord told me He was placing me in this ministry because He will work out my life's story to correlate with the name of the church. I got down on my knees in worship, praise, and thanksgiving to God! But I also said, "Lord, are You sure…?" I was tempted to remind Him of what my past says about me and the fact that I hadn't even been out of prison for two full years.

If I had reminded Him, He would have indeed remembered my prison experience, considering that He was molding me and using me during that time, but He would not have remembered the sins that got me there. When God forgives sins, He forgives them and remembers them no more (see Heb. 8:12). We have all heard the saying, "just forgive and forget." Only God can do both—and it's not like God is overtaken with Alzheimer's either. By His mighty power, He can control His omniscience not to go down my sinful historical road.

I did not wait to write this book until I had arrived at a place of "recognition" or destination where I could say, "Look where God has brought me from, and look where I am today—my promised land." Instead, I have put my trust in the Author of my journey— knowing that regardless of the obstacles or setbacks I may face along the way, He is more than able and faithful to perfect and bring to completion the good work He has started in me (see Phil. 1:6). He, not me or anybody else, is the Author and finisher of my faith (see Heb. 12:2). In this truth, there is great assurance.

My prayer is like David's: *"Uphold me according to Your word, that I may live; and do not let me be ashamed of my hope"* (Ps. 119:116). My hope is in God, the One in whom I put my trust. I don't have to wait until I "arrive" (whatever that entails) in order to tell my story and try to encourage others with it. I would rather start being helpful along the way. Though I may never get to a place of recognition or fame, which is certainly not my goal, my hope in writing this book is that some light would be shed on the darker side of the truth—in sinners and saints of old and sinners and saints today.

In Closing

Herein is the point of this book. Sinners need to know that saints are not perfect, sinless people, and we saints must stop giving them that impression. Saints also must be willing to demonstrate the restorative grace and love of God toward each other when one is overtaken in sin.

I have been both a sinner who became a saint and a saint who has sinned. I know I have and will continue to experience God's grace, justice, and mercy. I give God all the praise and the glory with thanksgiving for what He has done, for what He's doing right now, and for what He is going to do. I've begun a race that I must accomplish, come what may. There is no higher call or better purpose to fulfill here on earth. Though there may be multiple odds against me, I cannot retreat now nor surrender, for it is not God's will that I should care less about my present or abandon my future because of my past.

The Word of God declares that all things work together for good to those who love God, to those who are called according to His purpose (see Rom. 8:28), which indicates that God is not limited by any limitation that may come our way. The blood of Jesus still prevails; it can reach us down in the valley, and it can reach us up on the mountaintop—chances are we will experience both on our journey. Both the sinner and the saint have access to forgiveness in the blood. We all need it if we're going to make it.

David once said,

Blessed is he whose transgression is forgiven, whose sins is covered. Blessed is the man to whom the LORD does not impute iniquity, and in whose spirit there is no deceit (Psalm 32:1-2).

God will make every crooked path straight and every rough road smooth for the glory of His name (see Isa. 40:1-5; 42:16). Though we may have been beaten up by sin, afflicted and wounded, there is still mercy, grace, and unconditional love waiting for us. Jesus is waiting with arms open wide from the cross of Calvary.

Come, and let us return to the LORD; for He has torn, but He will heal us; He has stricken, but He will bind us up. After two days He will revive us; on the third day He will raise us up, that we may live in His sight (Hosea 6:1-2).

I can certainly say with assurance and conviction,

Indeed it was for my own peace that I had great bitterness; but You have lovingly delivered my soul from the pit of corruption, for You have cast all my sins behind Your back (Isaiah 38:17).

With full assurance and confidence in the God of my salvation, I will

Bless the LORD, O my soul; and all that is within me, bless His holy name! Bless the LORD, O my soul, and forget not

all His benefits: who forgives all [my] *iniquities, who heals all* [my] *diseases, who redeems* [my] *life from destruction, who crowns* [me] *with lovingkindness and tender mercies* (Psalm 103:1-4).

These Scriptures were a tangible part of my story. Never in my life has the Word of God been more real and precious to me, and it always will be! These were the Scriptures that spoke to the core of my spirit and have given me my own personal testimony that God is great, awesome, merciful, gracious, just, forgiving, and certainly not limited to limitations.

Lord Jesus, thank You for Your redeeming grace in my life! I still need to be a lot more than what I see. I refuse to stay where I am when You have so much more in store for me. You haven't given up on me, and neither will I give up on You. Thus, to and for Your glory and Heaven's reward, I continue my journey....

APPENDIX

Here are some books and Scriptures that I do recommend if you or someone you know is struggling with issues, especially of a sexual nature; they are also helpful if you want direction and encouragement as you pursue your destiny.

Arterburn, Stephen, Fred Stoeker, and Mike Yorkey. *Every Man's Battle.* Colorado Springs, CO: WaterBrook Press, 2000.

Arterburn, Stephen, Fred Stoeker, and Mike Yorkey. *Every Young Man's Battle.* Colorado Springs, CO: WaterBrook Press, 2002.

Osteen, Joel. *Starting Your Best Life Now.* New York, NY: Faith-Words, 2007.

Warren, Rick. *The Purpose-Driven Life.* Grand Rapids, MI: Zondervan, 2002.

Weiss, Douglas. *Sex, Men and God.* Lake Mary, FL: Siloam Press, 2002.

Keep in mind that the following Scriptures transcend the pornography battle to other areas of struggle: Galatians 5:1, 16-26; Luke 9:23; John 15:1-8; Romans 12:1-2; Second Corinthians 10:3-6; Ephesians 4:22-23; 6:10-18; James 4:7-8; First Peter 3:11; 5:8; Hebrews 12:1-6; Second Timothy 2:22; First Thessalonians 5:16-19.

CONTACT RAYMOND J. MOORE

Email: evidenceofgrace@hotmail.ca.

In the right hands, This Book will Change Lives!

Most of the people who need this message will not be looking for this book. To change their lives, you need to put a copy of this book in their hands.

> *But others (seeds) fell into good ground, and brought forth fruit, some a hundred-fold, some sixty-fold, some thirty-fold* (Matthew 13:8).

Our ministry is constantly seeking methods to find the good ground, the people who need this anointed message to change their lives. Will you help us reach these people?

> *Remember this—a farmer who plants only a few seeds will get a small crop. But the one who plants generously will get a generous crop* (2 Corinthians 9:6).

EXTEND THIS MINISTRY BY SOWING
3 BOOKS, 5 BOOKS, 10 BOOKS, OR MORE TODAY,
AND BECOME A LIFE CHANGER!

Thank you,

Don Nori Sr., Founder
Destiny Image
Since 1982